CW00829243

The author was born in Astley, Greater Manchester, in 1933, to a coal-mining family and blessed with a mother who was determined against the odds to give her two sons the best education she could muster. She worked tirelessly to achieve that end in days when grammar school was for the fortunate few—the very few in that local area.

Following back-breaking, early working experience in the mining industry, Donald eventually attained the status of Chartered Engineer, which eventually took him around the world as a consultant engineer to the pharmaceutical and confectionery industries.

These stories would have been impossible to relate without the unswerving support, trust and love from June, my lovely wife of sixty-plus years. She accompanied me, often reluctantly, with our two small children and performed a sterling job of family organisation, sometimes in pressurised circumstances and often in my forced absence. Absolutely full marks.

Donald Keith

TRUE TRAVEL TALES

(I'M NOT GOING THERE)

AUSTIN MACAULEY PUBLISHERS™

LONDON • CAMBRIDGE • NEW YORK • SHARJAH

Copyright © Donald Keith (2018)

The right of Donald Keith to be identified as author of this work has been asserted by him in accordance with section 77 and 78 of the Copyright, Designs and Patents Act 1988.

All rights reserved. No part of this publication may be reproduced, stored in a retrieval system, or transmitted in any form or by any means, electronic, mechanical, photocopying, recording, or otherwise, without the prior permission of the publishers.

Any person who commits any unauthorised act in relation to this publication may be liable to criminal prosecution and civil claims for damages.

A CIP catalogue record for this title is available from the British Library.

ISBN 9781528903066 (Paperback)
ISBN 9781528903073 (E-Book)

www.austinmacauley.com

First Published (2018)
Austin Macauley Publishers Ltd™
25 Canada Square
Canary Wharf
London
E14 5LQ

The author must pay tribute to the sterling work performed by his grandson Julian, who gave invaluable technical computer assistance towards the submittal of this work.

Table of Contents

The Adventure Begins (1963)   13

Introduction   14

Chapter One   16

Expanding Horizons (1963)

Chapter Two   20

Meeting Mr Hall (1965)

Chapter Three   25

Serving Mankind (1966)

Chapter Four   35

Do I Look Like Richard Burton? (1968)

Chapter Five   43

Always Listen to Your Wife (1972)

Chapter Six   45

Had a Nice Day, Love? (1970)

Chapter Seven   49

Shot in the Foot (1969)

Chapter Eight   50

These Foolish Things (1995)

Chapter Nine   52

Mao Tse Tung Was Here (1992)

Chapter Ten   74

The 23-Inch Seam (1959)

Chapter Eleven   78

The Way to Olampi (1972)

Chapter Twelve   86

Ah, Sweet Mystery of Life (1972)

Chapter Thirteen   88

A Nonsense of Norms (1957)

Chapter Fourteen   91

The Order of the Flattened Frog (1995)

Chapter Fifteen   95

A Case for Automation (1958)

Chapter Sixteen   99

Make Way! Make Way! (1996)

Chapter Seventeen   101

Economic Policing Made Easy (1971)

Chapter Eighteen   103

With Jesus as My Guide (1998)

Chapter Nineteen   107

The 200mph Wind (1972)

Chapter Twenty   111

The Land of Smiles (1978)

Chapter Twenty-One   119

The New Village Chief (1992)

Chapter Twenty-Two   122

All's Well That Ends Well (1974)

Chapter Twenty-Three   124

How to Handle Australians (1973)

Chapter Twenty-Four   128

Good Morning, Mr Smith (1969)

Chapter Twenty-Five   132

Yes Sir, Yes Sir (1971)

Chapter Twenty-Six   135

The Skateboard Waltz (1974)

Chapter Twenty-Seven   139

Where Is the Runway? (1985)

Chapter Twenty-Eight   142

Goodbye Gladys (1970)

Chapter Twenty-Nine   144

Knock It Down (1979)

Chapter Thirty   171

Unspoiled Pattaya (1966)

Chapter Thirty-One   176

Gainesville Intercontinental (1987)

Chapter Thirty-Two   179

A Narrow Escape (1977)

Chapter Thirty-Three   **184**

Always Drive on the Left (1985)

Chapter Thirty-Four   **185**

What About the Children? (1965)

Chapter Thirty-Five   **187**

An Invite to Lunch (1998)

Chapter Thirty-Six   **189**

Spooky

Obituary   **191**

The Adventure Begins (1963)

My transition from that point in my life to flying around the world in Mr William Wrigley's private luxury jet is catalogued in my autobiography, compiled for my heirs, and the following true episodes are but a few extracts from that journey.

The Adventure Ends (2002)

Introduction

Fifty-six years ago, I was one thousand yards underground in the middle of my nine-month compulsory hands-on coal mine training, rising at five am, down the mine at six, five or six days per week. I kept asking myself what I was doing there, I didn't belong there; me with my classical grammar school education, Latin and the arts, ambitions to become a journalist, what the hell was I doing there?

Working conditions at the three feet high coal face were horrendous, danger lurked all around, the dust, the screeching coal cutter and worst of all the claustrophobia. The miners had no time to worry about their trainee, I was given a shovel and told to get shovelling. It was horse work, and it played havoc with my lily white hands.

The reason was conscription. I had chosen to join an essential industry in preference to joining his majesty's post war forces in order to further my education combined with being able to contribute, however little, to the family budget.

The choice I made frequently weighed heavily on me during the quieter interludes as I walked the tunnels underground alone, sometimes in despair of my future. Not that I revealed any misgivings to my family, and certainly not to the hard bitten miners. Only eight months to go, then seven, I kept reminding myself, before I would begin the three years comprehensive business and management course, which together with my engineering college studies and completed five year mechanical apprenticeship would hopefully grant me acceptance into the professional engineering institution.

I encountered several post graduates who had made the same choice for the same reason, but the majority of these had fled the scene after one or two weeks, unable to come to terms with the harsh conditions. I almost joined the refugees when on one occasion, at the coal face, the roof of the tunnel without warning fell the four feet to the floor over a one hundred and fifty yard length with a resounding thud. It collapsed only ten feet behind the working miners, blasting me and the miners flat against the coal face. Many including myself suffered bruising, but fortunately no one was seriously injured.

Everything fell silent; no one spoke probably due to shock, then someone shouted through the impenetrable dust, "Everybody OK? Carry on." There was no time for your life to flash before your eyes as the saying goes, but had the roof fallen along the line of the coal face, we would all have needed very shallow graves.

Chapter One
Expanding Horizons (1963)

What strange forces dictate the path you are bound to take in life? Here was I, a fully trained and somewhat experienced engineer to the mining industry having been appointed chief engineer to the Co-operative Confectionery Division. What I knew about the manufacture of sweets and confectionery could have been written on a pinhead, and when I received the written job offer in the post, incredulous understates my reaction. Perhaps I had missed something in my education because I had attended several interviews where I had displayed in depth knowledge of the technical subject matter, being confident that I would land the job applied for, only to realise later that I had overplayed my hand. If you know too much about the job you are applying for, then the less chance you have of succeeding—no one wants to hire a smart ass. I never knew that.

The managing director who hired me was a charming Quaker gentleman dressed in Victorian fashion and who oozed superior aloofness. Arriving fresh from the mining engineering crew I had just left behind, who would have eaten him alive, I struggled in the first few weeks to come to terms with the aloofness of the MD as well as my other three Board members, my job being a new addition to that level. I should say at this juncture that I did manage to 'break in' the three other board members, but the MD was too far gone.

Nevertheless, always the gentleman and a fair and knowledgeable man from whom I learned a great deal. However, I was never able to become accustomed to the daily two to three hour lunches served in the palatial panelled board room. A menu fit to grace the finest restaurant, four courses naturally, sherry before, cognac afterwards, of course, served on the finest silver by properly attired waitresses. Who wanted to get back to the grindstone after that? I had to admit though that it beat a crunchy coal dust sandwich sitting on a rock. I joined in the cosy after dinner chats for a while not wishing to rock the boat, but soon I was unable to suppress the guilt I felt for too long and would always be the first to leave offering some usually valid excuse which seemed to puzzle the others.

It took me a while to get to grips with the variety of machinery used in manufacture and the multitude and variety of products, but after six months in the job, I felt comfortable technically and was coming to terms with my new found profession. Also, I had become to realise why the MD had hired me. He was forward thinking sufficient to realise that he needed to bring in new thinking and attitude to the factory to shake up the place which it badly needed, although I'm not sure he meant that to extend to the board room. However, in that regard, I can claim credit for radically reducing the frequency of three hour lunch breaks simply by making the others feel uncomfortable when I made my excuses, and two became the norm. My defining moment came when after six months in the job, the MD introduced me to his white elephant purchase which was in a separate building and under wraps. A large brand new fully automatic table jelly manufacturing machine purchased at great expense, designed by Cadburys, which had been sitting unused for over nine months because nobody could get it to work, not even the designer. Cooperative table jellies formed a substantial part of the business, and they were laboriously manually manufactured using a large array of cast iron moulding tables. The new machine occupied a fraction of the floor space, mixed moulded and cooled the jelly tablet ready to be ejected and wrapped using 60% less labour, all of which had been successfully commissioned with the exception of the ejection mechanism, which was a failure.

The few jellies it did manage to eject had ugly air holes within, rendering them unsightly and rejected. During the previous six months since my first day, no mention of this white elephant had been made to me either by the MD or any of my colleagues, but I now realised that I had been handed the poisoned chalice, the unmentionable subject even during the cognac course. Obviously, I would not be recording this if I hadn't solved the problem, but it is relevant that it was due to the training I had received in the mining industry that the toughest problem could be solved if enough thought was given to it. My overriding disadvantage however in this case was that I still knew bugger all about jelly manufacturing.

I spent many hours, lying on my back, studying the demoulding monstrosity. It looked wrong and over designed to my inexperienced eye. A month passed and although I did not have an alternative design in mind, I became ever more convinced that the principle was wrong and had the 'thing' removed and stored. I did consider calling in the scrap man but thought better of it in case I had to flee the scene. Eventually, regressing to my days in the design office and outside office hours due to the daily demands of managing my department, I arrived at an alternative concept of removing the jellies from the moulds without disfiguring their appearance. We constructed a prototype in our own factory workshop and installed it for a trial run. Soon, the ten girls and I who were on standby in case of failure, were up to our knees in orange table jellies because the take-off conveyor was overcome. A few refinements later, and we had a workable model.

The MD was somewhat pleased at the success, and although he kept his words to an absolute minimum due to his obvious training in aloofness, I realised that he was indeed pleased when the following morning, I received by telephone an invite to join him in his chauffer driven Rolls Royce on his twice weekly trips to collect the orders from Balloon St. Manchester. He chose to collect the orders in this fashion rather than delegate this menial task since a visit to head office meant meeting up with fellow aloofs of equal rank plus lunch in an even more palatial dining room. I made several such trips following the tumbling jellies, being now on the rotor with the other board members. It would be crass of me to say that these trips were anything other than enjoyable, but I did get a little concerned that the aloofness would rub off on me. However, the 23inch seam kept dragging me back to reality (story later). The designer of the original jelly de-moulding monstrosity telephoned me to invite me out for lunch. What! And miss the sherry and cognac—he must be joking.

What I was able to achieve in terms of innovative improvements to production machines and procedures did earn me a budding reputation in the industry, no doubt, influenced by the MD who had considerable influence in the trade. Of course, I was not aware of this, I was simply doing my best to establish myself in a new discipline—and I had an awful lot to learn. No performance reviews in those days, so you never knew the hierarchy thought of your competence or otherwise. The first indication I had that I must be doing something right was after eighteen months in the job, when I was approached by way of a personal visit from a senior executive from a major supplier of machinery to the confectionery industry. Had I considered my future options, and would I mind if he put my name forward to a company of international repute with whom he did business. I was certainly happy with my status quo and harboured no thoughts of moving on. I considered that I had still had much to learn before feeling confident enough to claim proficiency in confectionery production engineering. After all, I had been dealing with coal mining machinery not so long ago.

I was flattered to be asked naturally and decided to give the executive permission to proceed, but I agonised that evening over whether I had done the right thing. Little did I know then that my decision would change my and my family's lives forever.

Chapter Two
Meeting Mr Hall (1965)

Having been called to a preliminary interview over the telephone, I subsequently arrived at the office of the MD of Halls Confectionery in Whitefield to meet Ted Schofield, a large genial and intelligent man who was looking to appoint a Chief Engineer to his production unit. Halls had recently been acquired by the multinational Warner Lambert Co Inc. pharmaceutical manufacturers based in Morris Plains N.J. USA which I was aware of, but which was not raised at the interview, due, no doubt, to the fact that the position vacant was domestic based. The interview seemed to go well, but I heard no more of it, and three months had passed. I resigned myself to having fallen short, probably due to my lack of experience in the trade. Notwithstanding, I felt that I should have been formally rejected or otherwise, and on impulse, I telephoned Mr Schofield to enquire. To my complete surprise, he invited me to call at his office the following morning. He floored me with his opening statement when he said, "How would you like to live in Bangkok for a while." Totally unprepared for the question, I tried to conjure up mental images of Yul Brynner in 'The King and I' which I had recently seen at the Regal in Leigh. In 1965, Bangkok could as well have been on the moon as far as I was concerned. In fact, when I later told a school acquaintance that I was going to live in Bangkok, he said, "Where's that, down South?" I had not yet recovered fully from the initial question put to me when the door burst open and in strode a sprightly elderly gentleman who was introduced to me as Mr Hall of 'Mentho-Lyptus' fame. Long retired having sold out to the Americans, he was a typical Lancastrian character having scant regard for the fact that there was an interview in progress. "Art they an engineer?" he fired at me. "Yes Mr Hall," I replied, "I am a chartered engineer." He had obviously never heard of such a thing.

"Aye, but art any good wi machines?" Then, without warning, he tossed a ridiculously thick black passport to me across the table. "Have a look at that," he ordered. I felt a little embarrassed, but he insisted, so I gingerly picked it up and flicked through the pages, avoiding the personal data. Was there anywhere he hadn't been? "When theys got a passport like that they will have arrived. They looks alreet to me." Then he grabbed his passport and stomped out of the room. Ted Schofield burst out laughing.

"I wasn't expecting him today, but I think he likes you." When I had recovered my composure and heard more about the offered position, I arrived home to give my wife the news that I had provisionally accepted the position of project manager to build and manage a confectionery factory for Warner Lambert in Thailand, and that she and the children were coming too. Also, that I would be leaving for final interview in New York in two days' time. She kept me awake the whole night following, asking questions I couldn't answer, but by morning, she had a list of bedding items I had to bring from New York.

Flying from Manchester airport on a first-class ticket—only first and tourist available then—on the then revolutionary VC10, we touched down in Prestwick to fuel up for the Atlantic crossing. My head was filled with what I imagined to expect in American style interviewing of which I had no experience whatsoever. Would they understand my Lancashire accent, would my scant knowledge of confectionery production be a barrier? All manner of doubts filled my mind. This latter doubt worried me most, and I took to reading a technical book on the subject. Meanwhile, seated at the very front, I unexpectedly realised that all my fellow passengers including crew, had disembarked, and that I was the only person on the plane being absorbed in my reading. Suddenly, I was disturbed by the screeching sound of tearing metal which is a fearful noise. Standing to look into the galley area, I ventured in to see that the provisions loading door on the side of the plane was open and was being slowly torn off its hinges by the loaded pallet of a fork lift truck. The fuselage above and below the door was severely bulged as the substantial hinges refused to give way. I looked through the gaping hole to see that there was no one manning the truck. With a tremendous crack, the bottom hinge snapped, and I ran down the access steps intending to turn off the fork lift engine when I spotted the fork lift driver sprinting like mad towards the plane shouting to me not to touch the fork lift controls. I returned to my seat on the plane to await the inevitable inquest at which I would obviously be the key witness. Soon the first class cabin was filled with airport management and flight crew shooting questions at me—it was chaos. The ex-fork lift driver was trying to plead his case to everyone, and the airport manager sat down next to me taking notes to get my version of events, then the flight captain joined us taking his own notes. I was trying to make myself heard over the noise of everyone talking to everyone else. The VC10 was a spanking new jet liner, but it now had a big hole in its fuselage. Little wonder everyone concerned was grasping for an alibi. The commotion continued for over an hour when everyone including myself was ordered to retire to the airport departure lounge to join the rest of the stranded passengers. To rub salt into my wound, all the first class passengers were taken to a nearby castle resort for a gourmet lunch, that is, all except me, who had to sit in the departure lounge for six hours before the replacement plane arrived. The plane captain came to my seat once airborne to apologise that I had been overlooked for the castle trip due to the organiser taking one passenger from tourist class by mistake who carried the same name as mine. He gave me a bottle of good champagne as compensation. Was this incident an omen I wondered?

On reaching JFK New York I was met by Will Schultz, immaculately dressed in a silver suit, obviously expensive and designed to impress. What a charming man to whom I took an instant liking. Not at all the archetypal American I had only seen on the silver screen which was the only exposure I had experienced of the USA and its culture. Not at all. Softly spoken and very polite was Will. For reasons I can't explain, I conjured up a mental vision of Will standing in front of the mine shaft maintenance crew and quickly shook my head to banish such an improbable sight.

"First time in the US is it sir?" which I affirmed as we climbed into the first stretch limousine I had ever seen or knew existed. The car was bright red, the seats were blood red leather, and the dashboard, roof cover, and steering wheel were red. It was like the inside of a serious operation. *Everyone to their own taste*, I thought. We alighted at the entrance to the Waldorf Astoria which I did know of by reputation having seen it on films, but never in my wildest dreams had I expected to stay there. Magnificent interior. Will entertained me royally over that weekend and arranged to collect me on the Monday morning. Meanwhile, I tried to look as rich as possible amongst the hotel patrons, and I did have my best suit with me. I must have succeeded somewhat because descending in the lift next morning, I was accosted by the only other person in the lift. A little old lady dripping with jewels and obviously very rich, who asked me where I was from, then invited me to her residential suite to take a private breakfast. I politely refused but thanked her for her kind invitation. I was a little out of my depth because my mother had not warned me about little old ladies, only the young ones.

Will duly collected me the following morning and drove me to the headquarters of Warner Lambert International pharmaceutical company located in Morris Plains New Jersey. The interview went well, although some questions asked of me were unexpected such as had I ever been a member of the communist party for instance. One hour later, the panel announced to me that I had been successful in securing the appointment and introduced me to the Executive Project Manager for induction. I stayed at the Governor Morris Hotel in Morris Plains for one week to complete my induction and familiarise myself with the Thailand project. Having been forewarned about the heat and oppressive humidity of the Thai climate, I decided that I should have at least one tropical weight suit to take with me, consequently, I visited a gents tailors in the high street and explained to the assistant what I was looking for in an off the peg suit. Ten suits later, he told me that since I was not stock size, he could not oblige me. I told him that in the UK I had no such problem and that if any of his ready-made suits had fit me I would be seriously worried about my shape. I arrived home the following day carrying the voluminous project portfolio and a satisfactory contract of employment, not forgetting the also voluminous bedding items. I spent the following three months in the Hall Bros. factory assimilating the technicalities.

Events in the previous three months or so had overtaken my capacity to absorb somewhat, and both my wife and I needed a little time to come to terms with our new venture which seemed unreal and a little alarming. My wife at that time had never been out of the country, and we had scant knowledge of what to expect. However, we pulled ourselves together and made the necessary plans. I was to go alone to Bangkok to prepare the ground, and the family would follow one month or so later.

Should the reader get the impression that my wife was a willing participant in every one of our many moves around the world, then let me put the record straight. She was, and still is, a dedicated home bird, and on each and every occasion I had to break the news that we were moving countries, I got the same retort from her. It rings in my ears now as I write this—"I'm not going there!" or the more definitive version—"I'm definitely not going there!" There was only one title that I could give to this narrative.

Chapter Three
Serving Mankind (1966)

I was temporarily housed at the Imperial hotel having arrived in Bangkok six weeks prior to the arrival of my wife and family, when we would choose a more permanent home for our projected three year stay. I was already well known to the hotel staff after a couple of weeks and in particular to the Indian commissionaire stationed at the front entrance, who bent over backwards to please me, maybe because I was the only white face in the hotel, which was highly likely in 1966, or it could have been the tips. Nevertheless, in his gaudy over the top uniform, he presented a large commanding presence at the front entrance. A note was left at the hotel to advise me that my new company car would be delivered to the hotel car park that afternoon and that the keys would be left in reception.

I personally told the Indian to look out for the car and make sure it was parked safely and slipped him the usual tip. "Don't worry sir, don't worry sir I am here to serve mankind," bowing low as he spoke. Arriving back at the hotel that evening, I was greeted by the overexcited doorman in his flowing robes, who gave me the keys to my new car, ushering me into the car park to the white Ford. On reaching the car, he pulled from under his robes a large white cloth and proceeded to polish the gleaming paintwork with vigour. I sat in the car just to examine the controls. I had not driven an inch in Bangkok, and having seen the chaos on the roads en route to work, I had no intention of taking my new car for a drive that evening in the darkening gloom. Certainly not! The doorman however had other ideas as he rushed dangerously into the teeming traffic, arms held aloft to stop the oncoming hoard. I leapt out of the car to call him back from the dangerous road, where he had somehow got the normally aggressive traffic to halt, ignoring the shouted insults.

Back in my room, I settled down to write a few letters but couldn't find my Parker 51. I was sure it was in my inside coat pocket, but no, and I began to search my clothes and the room without success. *Must have dropped it in the new car when examining the controls*, I thought as I descended the lift. I had to pass the doorman on my way and received the usual bow as I passed by into the now darkened evening. As I entered the car and started the search, I became aware of someone polishing the car. It was the doorman, who flashed me a beaming smile through the window then dashed out into the traffic melee arms aloft. Again, I had to rescue him from the traffic amid droning car horns and shouts in Thai which could only have been insults. Back in the room, I conducted a thorough search but without result, and it seemed that my prized pen was indeed lost, although I had used it that day and felt sure that I had it on me when I arrived from work. I rang room service, and they loaned me a flashlight to enable a better search of my car.

This time however, I felt that I could not alert the effervescent doorman to my intentions and formulated a plan to evade him.

I emerged from my room looking left and right for an alternative way out of the hotel and found a 'services only' lift. Down I went to the lowest floor level and emerged into the hotel kitchens to the surprise of all the cooks, who started to laugh as I tried to find a route to the outside, opening doors hither and thither, until I finally found one which lead outside to the rubbish bins. The cooks stuck their heads out of the door to see what I was up to, laughing amongst themselves, but not challenging me. I was in a side alley amongst the bins in the dark as I tried to find my way to the front of the hotel in total darkness through dustbins and piles of rubbish. Eventually, I saw the lights at the hotel front and made my way to the corner which I peered around to see if the doorman was standing guard. No signs. Reminiscent of a spy movie, I dodged bushes and cars keeping a low profile to reach my car almost on my knees, negotiated the door lock with my key and squirmed into the driver's seat.

Triumphantly, I began to search the floor of the car using the torch and found my pen. I was about to leave when unbelievably someone was polishing my car. How did he spot me? But he had. Then, once more, the persistent fellow was in the road holding the heavy traffic at bay, smiling broadly over his shoulder at me and waving me into the road. I surrendered to the inevitable and started the car; I just could not disappoint the guy again, and not knowing where I was going, I drove very cautiously into the traffic chaos. I couldn't find the car lights switch, repeatedly turned on the screen wipers instead of the indicators and fiddled with the gearbox, but at ten miles per hour, I made it to the next left hand turning which I took, hoping that it would take me around the block and back to the hotel entrance. I was right, it did, so after my hundred yards test drive, I was back where I started, and who was standing at the roadside entrance? Yes, it could only be one person. When he saw my car approach, he waved wildly and ventured into the three lanes of traffic to open up a gap in the bumper to bumper vehicles to allow me to turn in. I began to realise what serving mankind was all about, and though I was at the hotel for six weeks, the Indian doorman's performance never varied from the excessive, sporting his ever present beaming smile. What a joy it must be, I thought, to be able to enjoy your work as much as he obviously did.

I was in Bangkok to construct an extension to the pharmaceutical manufacturing plant to house a new candy manufacturing facility producing Mentho-Lyptus throat and anti-congestion products which enjoyed massive popularity in Thailand at that time, plus other medicated products. The locals used the Mentho-Lyptus in various ways including the cooking of indigenous dishes or dissolved in hot water with a towel over their head to relieve congestion, also quite often you would receive your change from a shop purchase in Mentho-Lyptus lozenges instead of cash, particularly in rural areas. On one occasion, I heard from a fellow ex pat who joined a tiger hunt in the jungle, that as the hunting party were about to leave camp to begin the hunt one of the Thai guides stopped the party in their tracks to shout 'halt! I have forgotten my Mentho-Lyptus, I never go on a tiger hunt without my Mentho-Lyptus.' I thought what a slogan for an ad.

The factory was located in Paknam, some five or six miles into the Bangkok eastern suburbs, and I quickly became accustomed to the local way of doing things, thanks to my factory manager Pirawatt Panthawi, who was a Cambridge University engineering graduate and a fine fellow who I remain in contact with to this day.

When the time came to commission the manufacturing plant and equipment, it had not escaped my notice that that the factory workers wore totally unsuitable footwear to combat the very hot and dangerous molten candy produced by the large American made cooker or even remotely suitable for general factory conditions. Industrial footwear was unavailable in Thailand at that time, and I would need to import. The only suitable unisex footwear was the Lancashire clog having stout leather uppers and wooden sole. I contacted the Lancashire factory to airfreight a sample male and female set of clogs to Bangkok in the hope that a local cobbler could reproduce them.

The Bangkok shoemakers were totally baffled when I showed them the clogs, I therefore had no option but to order two hundred pairs of clogs in various sizes from my hometown clog maker which must have been the biggest single order he had ever received. When the workers were instructed to choose the size which fit them, I had overlooked the fact that the feet of the Thais were a slightly different shape to that of the European worker, but it never occurred to me that they could be different. However, in the interests of safety, I had no choice but to insist that the clogs must be worn.

The morning of the clog fitting should have been filmed. The scramble amongst the Thais to find a pair which almost fit, then they tottered into the factory like 150 Charlie Chaplin's. It took a while for the clogs to bed in, but many blisters later, they became accepted—in the interests of safety not fashion.

Every three months, I had to take the family to Penang Malaysia to renew our visas, which gave us a break from the oppressive humidity and heat of Bangkok. Residents visas were on a strict quota in Thailand, and it was twelve months before our name came up for consideration. The procedure to obtain resident status in 1967 was that I had to take $10,000 in cash to the nearest police station and give it to the desk sergeant who counted it before handing to me

28

the four residents books. Next, I had to take my whole family to the police headquarters and stand in a queue to see the chief of police. When our turn came up, we entered the chief's vast office containing one huge desk on a low dais covered almost completely with foliage and flowers. The police chief could just be seen peering through the jungle that was his desk. We stood before the desk staring upwards at his peaked cap in silence. It had all the ambience of a judge about to pronounce the death sentence. After what seemed like an age, the chief said in good English, "Do you enjoy living in Thailand?" Who was going to say no! We all had to say yes in turn. "Do you like the Thai people?" Same reply, both answers being truly spoken. I then reached up to give him the four residents books which he duly stamped using his ink pad and manual stamp, then pushed the books to the edge of the table through the foliage where I could reach them. The foliage closed back when he withdrew his hand, and we never did see his face.

We had been manufacturing product for launch for two weeks when the borehole well collapsed cutting off our only water supply. It was irreparable, and it would take three to four weeks to sink a new well. Pirawatt informed me that our only option was to hijack the water tankers passing the factory gate en route to outlying rural communities by waving money at the drivers. I didn't fancy the hijack business, but Pirawatt pointed out that he had done this successfully in a previous life in a similar situation. Still, I was adamant that I was not going to sanction robbing the villagers of their water. That was subsequent to Pirawatt having demonstrated on only one occasion that it did in fact succeed. Nevertheless, it was a serious setback to our timetable, not to mention our budget. I decided to approach the general manager of our adjacent Proctor and Gamble factory with a view to purchasing water from him by tapping into his borehole until we could sink our own, in quantities which would not compromise his own need, such as filling our storage tank overnight when he was not producing. He was a German national, and I visited him in his office. He flatly refused to come to our aid and was quite indignant that I had dared to make such a request of him. Scratching my head for a solution, I felt a little angry at being refused help from our neighbour, and gathering the factory engineering team together, I formulated a plan but did not issue direct instructions to carry it out. After all, it was tantamount to stealing, and I had been raised not to do that under any circumstances. I simply stated the fact that the German's borehole and storage tank was located only inches from our boundary fence, and it was much larger than our own, maybe twice as large, producing far more water than Proctor and Gamble would ever need and left it at that.

I was informed the following morning that during the night the mechanics had dug a shallow trench and connected us to the German's rising main. It was only a small pipe, but it was sufficient to keep us ticking, and they had done such a good job that there was no trace of the connection. Imagine my surprise! I did however instruct the team to install a water metre at our end so that if it was discovered we could pay for what we had taken. It never was, and three weeks later, our new borehole was on line, and the surreptitious line was disconnected this time under my direct instruction. The result was that we met our launch timetable, furthermore the German paid for his unjustified refusal to come to our aid, when shortly after this incident, his large Brylcreem storage tank, positioned just inside his warehouse door, burst overnight, and his car park got a hair do. How dare you suggest that we had anything to do with that—certainly not!

In any case, we didn't work regular night shifts.

The factory production was barely meeting the soaring sales, the main reason for this being our lack of sufficient steam raising capacity. I was aware of this deficiency in the early stages and had placed an order for a larger Cleaver-Brooks boiler from the USA which we now needed urgently but which had been stuck in Bangkok docks for the past two months. The forwarding agent in our Bangkok office was unable to clear it for delivery for a multitude of reasons, none of which made any sense to me.

It came to the point that at the following Friday, in the management meeting at the Bangkok office, I announced that I would go personally to the docks with Pirawatt to try to release the boiler. Everyone was horrified. In those early days no white man had ever been to Bangkok docks since he valued his sanity, not to say his wellbeing I was told.

Nevertheless, on the Monday morning at 9am, together with two carefully chosen security guards and with a flatbed truck following my car, we arrived at the dock gates. The barrier was closed, and two armed guards approached my convoy. When they saw me, they began a heated exchange of words in Thai shouting, I assumed, insults. There followed Mexican stand off until a queue of trucks had formed behind our flatbed. A mini riot ensued front and rear of us with the dock guards refusing to let us in and the truck drivers behind yelling at us to let them get past to get on with their daily job. The warring factions fell silent when a smartly uniformed dock official appeared, looking very important with his ornate baton, he spoke to me in perfect English as to what was going on, asking why I was there and what did I want. Next thing was my flatbed driver started brawling fisticuff style with the driver behind him until the guards separated them. I explained to the supremo, who I suspected had never been to the dock gates before, that I was there to collect our boiler which had been sitting in his store for two months, which was seriously limiting our ability to provide the Thai people with health products important to their everyday life. He raised the baton to his guards, and the barrier was lifted. That was only the beginning of a very long day and barely believable process to attempt to release the boiler.

Now in the clearing clerk's yard office, I presented all the relevant documents—and there were many. The clerks scrutinised the documents for fully two hours or more, leaving me saturated with perspiration in the searing heat and humidity, which did not seem to affect the Thais. "We need to see a sample of the boiler," said the chief clerk. I referred them to the pictorial catalogue showing all details. That was not good enough I was told, they required a physical sample. I explained that it was not possible to provide a sample of a boiler, but he would not be persuaded. "It is in our regulations that we must see a pre sample of every item we clear," the chief insisted with a look of triumph on his countenance.

Pirawatt did his best to explain in Thai the impossibility of the request, but to no avail. We were getting nowhere.

In frustration, I said that I would provide the chief with a sample of the boiler if he would allow me access to the warehouse and allow me to take the tools from my car.

No unauthorised person is allowed into the warehouse I was advised, at which point Pirawatt lost his Thai composure and berated the chief clerk with what I could only think was basic Thai abuse, whatever he told him however had the desired effect, and he handed the warehouse keys to me without a whimper. Pirawatt and I marched down the yard and entered the warehouse where we located our crated boiler. Risking the firing squad, we removed sufficient timber to give access to the water level sight glass and a sizable valve, both of which we removed. I handed the two items to the chief clerk on our return to the office, and it was obvious that he had no idea what they were. Nevertheless, he beamed a huge smile and pretended to examine the samples carefully. When he gave me the closed hands greetings of thanks, I was sure we had triumphed particularly when he began to fill in what looked like clearance documents.

Not so! The assistant clerk who was studying the catalogue interrupted the form writer telling him that the boiler could not be released because it was against the law to import telecommunication equipment without a special import licence.

We had, by that time, spent five hours in the furnace they called the yard office, and the heat and humidity was really getting to me, however, I made the effort to control myself and blessed the good Lord that I could not speak Thai at that moment, instead I could not suppress a muffled laugh at the suggestion. The clerk had noticed in the literature that the boiler was of multi tube construction, and to him, in those days, tubes was the common name for diode valves. Pirawatt did his best to explain the misinterpretation, but it fell upon deaf ears. The chief clerk suddenly remembered that there was a form for this situation and produced from his dust laden folders a document headed The Ministry of Communications and asked me to complete the form promising that I would not construct a radio transmitter from the water tube boiler. I filled the form full of the most nonsensical technical jargon imaginable, signed my name to it and gave to the beaming clerk. Had we cracked it? No, we hadn't. There was the matter of import duties to be settled which had to be paid before the boiler left the docks. I had come with sufficient cash dollars to more than cover the official duty rate for boilers, having anticipated this request. The clerks however demanded that the item should be classified under telecommunications equipment, which carried twice the rate of duties than did boilers. "Not that again," I groaned.

Pirawatt whispered to me that it was accepted procedure to reward the clerks for their valuable assistance in allowing goods to be removed from the docks. However, I was determined that I was not going to do that, which caused Pirawatt to roll his eyes and wipe his brow. I decided to leave the financial transaction for Pirawatt to negotiate with the two robbers, and when the interchange reached fever pitch, I interceded by offering to leave all the dollars I had with Pirawatt if the clerks would allow me to load the boiler on to my flatbed truck . To my surprise, the clerks agreed and gave me a clearance ticket to do just that, at which point I made myself scarce and left to organise the loading. Dusk was approaching as I commandeered a passing lift truck and loaded the crate on to my flatbed.

Pirawatt joined me in the flatbed and gave the remaining cash to me which I didn't bother to count, then we drove to the gate. Following a slanging match between my Thais and the gatekeepers, the barrier was finally raised, and we were away. It was too dark to make it to the factory that day, so we parked up the flatbed overnight leaving behind our hired guards to ensure it would still be there the following morning.

When the boiler arrived at the factory the next day, you would have thought we had just won the FA cup. The whole factory turned out into the courtyard to clap and cheer. Needless to say, I did not visit the docks again, but I did notice an improved performance from my purchasing and clearing department.

During the commissioning of the factory we accumulated some five tons of scrap Mentho-Lyptus which was not reclaimable. No facilities existed then other than burning or burying such waste. I got the maintenance crew to dig a deep hole in the lawn behind the factory, and we buried the scrap, then levelled out and re-turfed the lawn.

Six months later, Pirawatt came to my office to tell me that a new hill had sprung up overnight behind the factory. Sure enough, the gases had pushed up a sizable hillock, some five feet high. I had two steel pipes driven into the mound and lit the emitting pressurised gas. The flares burned for a full day resembling an oil strike. Only then could we safely flatten out the mound.

We enjoyed traveling the country whenever the opportunity arose. Pattaya beach, then an unspoiled paradise, the river Kwai at Kanchanaburi and the notorious Burma railway and its war graves, the fantastic rose gardens. We were also fortunate to witness the Royal Boat Festival having seats just behind the royal box. I didn't know until that time that Pirawatt's uncle was their equivalent of our First Lord of the Admiralty. Why didn't he tell me that at the docks? The river festival was an unforgettable occasion, a once in a lifetime opportunity to witness the long held traditions of ancient Siam.

To cap our unforgettable stay in Thailand, and not long before we left, I was badly bitten on my calf by a neighbour's dog while rounding up our children who were playing in the soi (Side Street.) Blood was drawn, and the obvious worry was rabies, so I naturally telephoned the neighbour to get information on the dog. The telephone was answered by a very aristocratic male English accent who told me that the dog was fully protected and that there was no need to worry, but should I decide to sue him I should take into account that he was the Attorney General.

June had cried all the way travelling to Thailand she told me, and she also cried all the way out.

Chapter Four
Do I Look Like Richard Burton? (1968)

I had been pre warned about the real dangers abounding concerning an ex pats' life in Manila prior to the family relocation there from Bangkok. Still, it was but a six month contract to 'upgrade the performance from the company factory' there, to be followed by a return to Europe and home leave. I offered to the family that heeding the warnings given, they could return to the UK, and I would complete the assignment alone, but they had enjoyed Bangkok so much that they opted to accompany me to Manila.

Having had our pre-departure lunch in the Bangkok Erawan coffee shop, we returned to our room to organise our previously packed luggage comprising some twelve suit cases and assorted bags—those were the days when you could take mountains of luggage on a plane, particularly if flying first class—when I noticed that protruding from a zipped up flight bag was an expensive looking umbrella handle. Not recognisable to myself or my wife, I withdrew the umbrella which had a quality leather cover and ornate handle and was about to examine it when a knock at the door said that our taxi awaited. I pushed the umbrella back into the flight bag, and we scampered down to our taxi. On arrival at Manila airport, I collected the luggage when I noticed that the umbrella had disappeared. What we had inadvertently smuggled into Manila that day I will never know, but had we been caught with it, I would have had no defence. Cold sweat time when I realised how we had been set up.

Gus Figueredo, the US CEO and his wife met us and drove us to San Lorenzo precinct and a banana shaped but quite splendid house, one of twenty or so such houses within a walled enclosure having single in and out barrier and armed guarded accesses. In front of the house were two motorcycle policemen watching our arrival which I thought was unusual but was assured by Gus that they were assigned full time to patrol the streets inside the walled area which put me on my guard immediately, wondering if the warnings I had received were underestimated. I kept my apprehension to myself not wishing to unnecessarily alarm my wife, it was early days I told myself. My apprehension was further heightened however when we entered the master bedroom which sported a nine feet wide bed behind which was a large gun rack and a button console from which the curtains could be drawn, various lights could be operated, and telephones and intercom were placed. The guns had been removed, but it set me wondering if the previous occupants would have had need to use them. The rooms throughout the house were opulently furnished, and my family liked it inside and out which was the main thing. I privately formed the opinion that the house was banana shaped so that intruders could not get a clear shot, but didn't express my feelings, and furthermore I had to agree that despite its unusual shape it was a high quality residence. Gus then revealed to us that the house belonged to Dodge Laurel, the then Philippine champion formula 1 driver who had been killed in the Macau grand prix three months earlier, when he had managed to rent it from his wife for the period we were to stay. That explained the formula one car parts which littered the vast garage behind the house, including a full chassis. Also, it went some way to explaining the security measures within and surrounding the house since he must have been something of a target for the shadier members of the community.

Makati, the suburb of Manila we were in was undoubtedly the upmarket part of town, with a sizable population of well-heeled locals and ex pats living in lavish style judging by the impressive houses around—stately would be an understatement in describing some of these. All were located within similar walled and secure enclosures similar to the one we were in, beautifully landscaped.

The shopping areas were numerous and similarly upmarket including supermarkets which at that time were lacking in the UK.

The area had been Americanised to coin a phrase, and facilities were good around the area. Within two weeks of arriving and getting to know the area a little better, I began to wonder if the scare warnings had been exaggerated by our well-meaning friends in Bangkok—but I hadn't been to the city centre yet. I had need to do so soon in order to greet a German engineer staying at a hotel in town. I did not employ a driver at that time so not knowing the city streets at all I followed directions from Gus who stressed to me not to drive with any car windows open due to the city boys 'game' involving shooting blowpipe arrows into drivers heads through car windows

Taking the hint, I finally found the hotel, but not before I had been stopped by a policeman at a junction traffic light who instructed me to lower my window, then said that it would be in my best interest if I would purchase from him a loyalty card. Asking him why I should need to do so, he replied that if I was involved in a road accident of any kind and I flashed this card to the police, the accident would automatically be the other drivers fault, irrespective of the circumstances. I considered this to be a good investment considering the chaotic road traffic and handed over five US dollars to receive a credit sized card headed 'friend of the police.' I thought it might come in useful when I got back to the UK. What would happen if the other driver also had the same card was not explained properly to me, but I reasoned that a draw was better than nothing.

I met up with my German visitor and over coffee learned that it was his first trip to the Far East, and he was excited to be there. We discussed the business in hand, then decided to venture out of the hotel to view our surroundings a little. As we jogged down the ten or so steps into the street, a man came running from around the corner, firing a hand held machine gun from which he was spraying bullets as he ran. Shooting at no one in particular, he was yelling in the local tagalo, people were diving for cover, and I pulled my guest to the pavement since there was no time to run back up the hotel steps. Finally, the man disappeared down a side street, and we got to our feet to be amazed to find people just walking around as though nothing had happened. Back in the hotel, the concierge showed no concern at the incident and was more concerned about whether we had enjoyed our stay. "Must be a daily occurrence," I said to the German who was still in a state of shock.

The factory management staff made me most welcome, and I was able to solve some of their long standing production related problems, and they were most appreciative and easy to get along with. They related my advice as 'grandfatherly' advice as distinct from advice from an American which they termed fatherly advice. USA they said was the son of the UK, and the Philippines was the son of the USA. Certainly, I had not thought in these terms, but they were convinced that that was the case. I had no cause to argue the case but for some reason it made me feel older than I was.

It was at the Pasig Rizal factory that I met the slowest walker I had ever met. He was the young factory engineer, and he had the most unusual walking action of anyone I have ever met. He seemed to take a normal stride when walking beside you, yet you quickly left him behind even walking at normal pace. I tried to analyse why this was but was never able to do so. It was certainly a disadvantage when rushing to sort out an emergency breakdown—he would have been of interest to someone researching human kinetics.

While walking through the warehouse with the factory manager one morning, we were startled by what sounded like a hornet zipping across our path causing us to recoil a little. Then I noticed a tiny waterfall of white sugar falling from pallets of sugar sacks. Suddenly, more zipping sounds at which point Nario dragged me to the floor—someone was shooting bullets through the cladded wall and they were whizzing past a metre in front of us. We literally crawled back to the office and raised the alarm by calling the local police station who told us that armed officers would be sent.

However, before they arrived, a team of volunteers from the factory offered to find the culprit and judging where the shooter might be from the numerous bullet holes in the wall, the men set out across the adjacent field to find him. It was somewhat foolhardy of them unarmed as they were, but as I watched from a safe distance I could see that they were in fact crawling through the grass towards where the shooter was still firing at the factory. The volunteers crawled out of our sight over a low hillock, and we heard shouts and sounds of scuffling, and the team reappeared dragging along the disarmed shooter. This raised cheers from the group of workers watching from a safe distance as they dragged the offender to the factory forecourt at which point the police arrived in their jeep and roughly dumped the deranged offender in the rear seat and drove away. The culprit turned out to be an ex-employee at the factory who had been dismissed the week prior to the incident and who resided in the nearby barrio. We never did hear anything further on the matter. I decided to recheck my insurance cover.

As a family, we were escorted around the tourist destinations on Luzon Island, volcanos, beaches and the famous Pansagnanj falls which, when I received the invitation, I wrongly assumed to be a cultural centre requiring dress suit attire.

On arrival, I was surprised to see everyone in beachwear. That is all except myself and family who were dressed to the nines. I wore smart tropical suit and tie, and my wife was suitably matched. We imagined that the tour involved a leisurely cruise down the river to view the falls. Then we discovered that the trip involved the four of us sitting in a roughly made canoe with water lapping inside being physically carried on the shoulders of two strong young men in loincloths up a boulder strewn sixty degree canyon down which rushed the falls as a rapids. They dragged us over boulders and rocks to the top using brute strength where we sat beside the serene lake which was feeding the falls, then we were allowed to rest to take refreshment available from vendors. The scenery was superb, and the children could bathe or fish the lake—all very enjoyable despite my damp trousers and socks. I remember thinking it would at least be easier for the two boys to carry us down the canyon. You are probably ahead of me but yes, we had to shoot the rapids to get back to the bottom. The narrow rapids were frightening to look at, zigzagging down the boulder strewn canyon, but the two boys said that we could trust them to make the descent safely. I was convinced, but not my wife, but since it was the only way down I finally managed

39

to get her into the canoe. That descent will be etched on my memory forever, trying to hold my wife and children within the shallow canoe, water splashing over us, and worst of all dodging the rocks and boulders as we descended at breakneck speed. It was like watching the close up of a disaster movie. The skill and strength of the two paddlers was very impressive, fending off rocks and boulders by flashing their stout paddles left and right. The force of the descending water did the transporting, and as we emerged into the gently flowing river, the feeling of relief was overwhelming. The experience was strictly for thrill seekers but not family entertainment—at least not in 1968. However, I must hold the record for the best dressed man ever to make that trip—something I never checked on. Our favourite out of town trip was to Baguio high in the northern mountain of Luzon, which we were told at that time held the world record, twenty four hour rainfall record at thirty three inches. What a magical place it turned out to be, although the mountain roads to it were a test of courage. The forested mountain scenery is outstanding, and the pure cool mountain air is like wine to breath, blessed relief from the heat and humidity of Manila. The morning sunrise is an unforgettable experience, rainbow colours reflecting on the mist, you just run out of superlatives, and we braved the dangerous roads more than once to relive the experience. It was also head hunter territory, and on one occasion, as we browsed the small town open market, we encountered a hill tribesman who frightened the life out of my wife since he wore no clothes at all except for a battered straw hat and a rope belt around his waist from which dangled a few shrunken human heads and a panga—incidentally, the heads could be purchased on one specialist market stall. We had been warned that head hunting was still prevalent amongst some primitive tribes living around that area, and the market trader was adamant that his shrunken heads were genuine. I must say that they certainly looked genuine. My wife was horrified when I told her that we must have bumped into the wholesaler. No, we didn't purchase one, but we had a hard time keeping our five and ten year old away from that stall, which was enough to give you nightmares.

The Philippine people loved celebrities, it is in their nature; they also love music and singing, and we had many enjoyable musical evenings out in the city. Two incidents occurred which illustrated their appetite for the famous. At this juncture, I have to inform the reader for no other reason than to explain that my wife, in looks, hair and dress was the double of Elizabeth Taylor who was at that time all the rage with film fans. She will not thank me for revealing this because she has always been very reserved in nature, but there was no doubt about it. One day we were walking through the classier shopping area just browsing the windows, and I was lagging behind my wife who was fifty yards ahead. Suddenly, all the shop girls and other shoppers were running out of shops and surrounding my wife shouting that Elizabeth Taylor was in town. There was quite a crowd gathering, and I ran to force my way through to June who was being manhandled and pushed around. I shouted over the din that she was not Elizabeth Taylor, but the crowd wouldn't have it, and the situation was getting out of hand. The only thing I could think of at the time was that I was in no way the double of Richard Burton and shouted this to the crowd as loud as I could. Eventually, the crowd got the message and they began to drift away, and though she was shaken up, my wife recovered her composure, and we beat a swift retreat.

The second incident was a little scarier. We were in a night club in the city centre together with three company managers who had checked their guns in to the cloakroom attendant as was required and who were entertaining us for the evening. We were seated around a table positioned on a low dais. Other tables around the dimly lit club were at differing heights which was a feature of the décor. We were enjoying a drink chatting amongst ourselves when a suited member of staff walked up to our table carrying a magnificent large bouquet of flowers and presented it to my wife with compliments. At first, she refused to accept it since she said to the man that she didn't accept flowers from a stranger. The flower bearer then said, "I would advise you to take them madam, the gentleman who sent these is seated high up there," as he pointed to a table high across the other side of the club. "Please acknowledge." As we looked skywards across the club, we could see four men seated around a table one of whom our party recognised as the most powerful mafia boss in Manila. One of the men had binoculars, and they had mistaken June for Elizabeth Taylor. The mafia boss raised his hand to our table, and all the men raised our hands in acknowledged unison. The flower carrier then re-presented the bouquet to June saying, "Flowers for a beautiful lady." At his point, we persuaded June to raise her hand in acknowledgement. We beat a hasty retreat at the first opportunity, not wishing to be invited to the sky-high table.

One evening, we were sitting in our banana shaped lounge room watching television where we had eleven channels to select from, whereas back in the UK at that time we only had three. The children were watching the Uncle Bob children's show which was very popular with all the kids. Uncle Bob was a US soldier who had stayed behind after the war to run his own TV channel mainly directed towards children, cartoons, games and the like. Both children were laying on the carpet head propped up in their hands laughing and chattering along with the show. Wife and I were reading newspapers I seem to recall, when I lowered my newspaper to notice that my son was not there. I dropped my paper intending to find him when to our complete amazement, he walked on to the television screen and began talking to uncle Bob who introduced him as a guest from Manchester England who wanted to play his guitar for the children, which he did. It was less than ten minutes before that he had been sprawled on the carpet in front of us.

It transpired that watching the programme ten year old Peter suddenly decided that he wanted to meet uncle Bob in person, so he left the lounge unnoticed by us and commandeered my newly hired driver to drive him to the TV station which we later discovered was less than a three minute drive away from the house. Full marks for initiative, but we had to read the riot act to him on his return since his security had been compromised, and he had to be made to see the danger in that.

Chapter Five
Always Listen to Your Wife
(1972)

The relatively cool Taipei winter was upon us, and it was time to wheel out the sweaters and such like. Not that the weather was uncomfortably cold—except that is for the mountain heights of Yang Ming Shan overlooking the city below, which was the location of our company assigned temporary home .We had become accustomed to the multitude of deadly snakes surrounding us, also the fact that our garden served as a cemetery for the locals, plus the fact that we were the only Catholics living on the Methodist Theological College enclosed compound. No one seemed to mind as long as we contributed to the numerous collections to good causes.

While shop gazing down town one evening around the perfectly safe streets, even at 10pm, I advised my wife that I needed to buy a warm suit since tropical suiting was all I possessed. Despite displaying shock and awe at the statement, she followed me into the tailor's shop and joined me in feeling at the numerous bolts of cloth on display. Feeling for something warm to the touch notwithstanding the colour or price, I chose a subdued beige and grey tartan bolt standing out from its contemporaries which were all dignified business dark blue and grey. It should be pointed out that this would be the first time I had unilaterally chosen my own suit without substantial input from my wife who had superior dress sense, freely admitted by me. The shock and awe returned to my wife's face at the choice, and she vowed that she would never walk beside me if I wore it. The Chinese tailor had a similar look on his face and tried to persuade me to consider his choice of a dark blue serge made in Huddersfield—Huddersfield Japan that is. Not to be swayed, the warmth of the tartan won the day, and I was duly measured for trousers and jacket.

Two weeks elapsed following which I told my wife that we had been invited to dinner at the apartment home of the Chinese contractor who was constructing the factory I was in Taiwan to oversee. This was a very unusual invitation at that time since the Chinese operated on a strictly private basis, and to be asked to meet his wife and family was something of a surprise and honour.

The evening of the visit was a particularly cold one, and I, despite protracted protest, donned the warm tartan suit. The grief continued in the taxi going down the snaky mountain road, and on until we reached the sixth floor apartment door. Mr Robert Sih opened the door, looked me up and down, and having seen me dressed only in business attire, looked a little taken aback at seeing the tartan clad visitor. He quickly recovered and ushered us into his living room where all his furniture was covered in the same tartan material. I sat on the settee where I immediately disappeared from sight, and my wife looked too stunned to utter a word. No comment was made whatsoever by Mr Sih or his wife, who were much too polite to mention the obvious, but the interchange conversation was a little strained on both sides. He was obviously wondering why he, or rather his wife, had been so stupid as to cover their furniture in tartan moquette which the all-knowing westerners were making suits out of. The journey back up the mountain was memorable.

Chapter Six
Had a Nice Day, Love? (1970)

My workday morning routines were well established. I would rise at 6:30am, breakfast at 7am prepared for me by Didi, the cook, by which time my driver would have cleaned and readied the car to take me to Taipei rail station to catch the 8am train to Neili. This format was carefully planned and was well practised and successful. Chen would then return to base to ferry my wife to wherever she needed to go on the day.

The Taiwanese rail service was excellent regarding timekeeping and passenger comfort and service, and on that particular morning, I was unsurprised at seeing the train standing at the usual platform. I boarded, took a seat and awaited the guard as was routine to purchase a ticket and offer me the *China Post*—English version.

Before the guard had arrived, the train pulled out of the station, and as the large station clock sailed past his window, I noticed the hands spot on 8am. The guard arrived, and I requested a ticket to Neili, but the guard shook his head and looked quizzically at me. I repeated the request, but the guard gabbled something in Chinese while shaking his head. Across the aisle, a Chinese passenger overheard the goings on and spoke in English to me to inform that the train I was on was the nonstop express to Kaoshiung. He went on to explain that the large signs in Chinese on the platform they had just left were to advise travellers that all trains were running one hour behind schedule due to work on the line. Neili is some thirty miles down island—Kaoshiung is two hundred and fifty or more, being almost the furthest point at the southern tip. Nothing could be done—no choice but to sit it out. One act of grace was provided by the guard when he charged me only the fare to Neili.

Three hours plus later the train pulled into Kaoshiung harbour, and I sought out the local station master to seek advice, but he couldn't be traced. No one spoke English, and I was unable to make the station staff understand my predicament. Finally, after waving my Neili ticket under the nose of a small man in rail uniform pushing a baggage trolley, who turned out to be the station master, and after much unintelligible conversation and gesticulating, I was directed to a train standing in the station. With cries of Neili and finger pointing by what was now a small crowd of station staff, I ran to the standing train and jumped on. I realised immediately that the train I was on was no luxury model, but there was a central aisle with tables and bench seats on either side, so I slid into a window seat, glanced at my watch showing twelve noon, then started to read my *China Post*.

Very soon after, the train began to fill up, and the seats and aisle became crowded with malodorous local farm workers male and female, some very poorly clad .The three vacant seats around my table were occupied by two young boys, opposite and seated next to me was an old lady with a large carpet bag across her knees. I tried to look as inconspicuous as possible with my pin stripe suit, silk tie and executive briefcase, hiding myself as much as possible behind my *China Post*. Everyone standing in the aisle was craning their necks to get a good look at the alien riding on their constantly stopping train taking them to work, or wherever. After a while, the old lady unwrapped a large sandwich and started to eat it. I could see out of the corner of my eye that the sandwich was so large as to require the lady to use both hands to hold it. The lady then broke off a piece of the sandwich, unzipped the carpet bag a little and pushed the piece into the bag and zipped it closed quickly. This was repeated a few more times when on the last manoeuvre and without warning, my newspaper was torn to shreds as a huge white gander's head and neck shot through it under my nose. With admirable reflex, I grabbed the beast's neck with both hands and attempted to force the gander back into the carpet bag, but the strength of the gander trying to force itself out of the bag was considerable. Feathers flew everywhere, small downy feathers which stuck to everything they touched.

The crowded compartment was in uproar with laughter, and I was not winning the wrestling match with the gander which had released one wing from the carpet bag and was flapping wildly. The old lady could be of no assistance and was near to hysteria when a farmer came to my assistance, and between us we managed to get the gander back into the bag and zipped him in to loud cheers from the crowd. My business attire was now covered in white down feathers which refused to be removed, and I had no option except to sit tight but had to smile back at the highly amused onlookers. The train ground to a halt in what to me seemed a reasonably large station and having endured an hour on the stop start local hopper, I decided to alight and take my chances of catching a faster train back to Neili. Repeat performance in trying to get the station staff to understand—this was after all 1970, and Taiwan was still firing daily shells across the straits into communist China and was just emerging into the outside world. This time the station staff pointed to a train which was parked on the opposite line in a side shunt, not at a platform at all. Puzzled at this, I hesitated since it meant jumping on to the tracks to reach the train. However, such was the insistence of the Chinese that I jumped on to the track, took the bull by the horns and sprinted across tracks to the standing train, which as I neared, started to move very slowly forward. With some difficulty, I managed to mount the high first step to the moving door and wrestled the archaic handle open to board. Walking down the central aisle, I found an empty table and sat down, panting for breath, with the other passengers on the train obviously wondering where this alien had sprung from. The fact that I was covered in white feathers probably added to their incredulity.

At least the new train was heading in the right direction and was moving at speed with few stops. I glanced at my watch, estimating that with a bit of luck I might make it to the office before the factory closed for the day. The train finally pulled into Neili station at 4:45pm, and I had 15 minutes to get to my office. A quick dash to the taxi rank, which only boasted one taxi ever, but it was there, and I murmured quadi to the driver who reached the factory in a record seven minutes. My secretary greeted me with her usual beaming smile and gave me a long list of missed calls without a mention of why I was dressed as an eider duck. Just another day at the office.

Chapter Seven
Shot in the Foot (1969)

Standing in the longish queue awaiting passport departure at Hong Kong airport, I stood immediately in front of a very large and tall Texan man dressed in full regalia—white rhinestone decked suit, white cowboy Stetson and boots, all tanned and lovely. Suddenly, the Texan started to boast in a loud voice, shouting that although Hong Kong was 'a fine little town', it could not hold a candle to Texas where the skyscrapers were twice as high, the roads twice as wide and went on to describe everything in Texas as being bigger and better. The Chinese staff were obviously embarrassed and uncomfortable at the outburst as was the queue. Immediately, behind the boaster stood a skinny 5 feet nothing man dressed immaculately in black London financial district attire complete with bowler hat and black brolly. The Texan turned to the diminutive banker and clamping a huge hand on his shoulder said in his booming voice, "And where are you from son?" The man said, "Texas." The queue and the Chinese dissolved.

Chapter Eight
These Foolish Things (1995)

It was that every Sunday my wife would prepare a picnic hamper, and we would resort to the Nairobi National Park to marvel at the sights and enjoy our lunch at a designated picnic site, just the two of us. Knowing the park layout well by then, we did our tour and eventually arrived at the picnic site which unusually was deserted apart from ourselves. I got out of the Land Rover Discovery and walked to the rear to scout the area for any wildlife, in particular baboons, which were drawn to the picnic site for leftovers and rubbish bins. Satisfied that the short savannah grass and bushes were clear of nuisance, I opened the large rear door and reached in to remove the hamper.

In an instant, something heavy and hairy landed partially on my back and the open car door causing me to lash out my right arm forcefully in a reflex action. This dislodged the intruder, and I turned around to be face to face with a male baboon showing his impressive fangs— mouth open wide. Adrenalin charged, I attempted to push the hamper back into the vehicle, but the baboon leapt at the basket, and a fist fight ensued. It never occurred to me in the heat of the moment that the fangs could inflict serious damage, only that I had to get the rear door shut to prevent the theft of my lunch.

Otherwise it was a fair fight between two primates. Having struck a hefty blow to the baboon's chest which backed it off a little, I was able to close the door and quickly dash around to the driving seat to shut myself in.

My wife seemed totally oblivious to the battle going on behind her, leaving me to reflect on what could have been and how foolish it was to have engaged a male baboon in mortal combat without some kind of weapon. Not to be outdone, the baboon jumped on to the back of the Discovery as it moved away and spread itself over the rear window, clinging on for dear life. Any doubt that it was a male baboon were dispelled by its long male member being pressed flat drooping down against the rear window, which started my wife off in hysterical laughter. I weaved the car side to side to dislodge the animal, but it clung on tenaciously. Only when the car reached a rocky section of track did the baboon finally let go. Thinking about the incident later, I realised how lucky I was to have escaped with a few scratches, though I did concede that the baboon did deserve half a prawn sandwich for persistence.

Chapter Nine
Mao Tse Tung Was Here (1992)

Lawrence Li had said that the next time I was in Hong Kong, I should look him up. Lots of acquaintances say that in the business world, few actually expect you to do so due to other persistent pressures. On this occasion, things were different. I was in the city with my family and between contracts, and the opportunity to ring Lawrence presented itself.

"Would you like to build me a factory in China," was the greeting as we met in his plush penthouse office overlooking the spectacular harbour front. China was closed for business at the time and certainly westerners were largely shunned and distrusted as subverts to the communist ideal. I had held an ambition to visit Shanghai from my youthful readings but did not disclose this to Lawrence, and politely declined the offer. This was strictly a social visit, and the meeting continued in that vein, culminating in dinner with the family, and a jolly time was had by all. There was a half promise from me to reconsider the China proposal said during the 'good nights.'

The following morning, a car and driver arrived at my hotel to take me to the penthouse for 'amicable discussions,' and these ended with my agreeing to at least taking a trip to visit the proposed China site with no obligation. How Lawrence managed to obtain tickets for the China Airways flight I never knew, since they were like gold dust to obtain at that time, particularly for the likes of me, for whom it would have been personally impossible,

The early morning ferry trip up the Pearl River to Guangjou (Canton) was very pleasant and put me in good spirits to face the rest of what I knew would be a long journey. I was met at the ferry terminal by a Li confidant who drove me to the airport to embark a plane for Nanjing—a two-hour hour flight by China Airways. As far as I could see, I was the only non-Chinese aboard, but I would have wished for at least another madman 'farang' to be on board as a small measure of comfort that I was doing the right thing. On arrival, I joined the throng of jostling passengers at the luggage collection area, where after a one hour wait, the luggage finally arrived, loaded into the open back of a tipping lorry as used on building sites. The truck reversed into a caged enclosure where it simply tipped everything on to the concrete floor in a huge heap. They then locked the cage door after the lorry drove out. Some thirty minutes later, with the passengers peering through the wire cage, the officials unlocked the cage and jumped out of the way of the onrushing crowd. It was mayhem, with everyone attacking the heap of luggage, throwing cases and bags around searching for their own. I couldn't stand on ceremony and joined in the free for all. After what seemed like an age, I finally reached the customs desks and was greeted by stony faced officials who looked at me suspiciously, then went through all of my luggage with a fine tooth comb and confiscated my favourite letter opener as being a dangerous weapon.

Exiting the terminal, I searched the waiting crowd outside—a sea of faces—looking for any sign that someone was there to greet me as Lawrence promised—nothing obvious, just Chinese character placards and numerous photographs of relatives or friends. The crowd started to thin out, but still no recognizable sign that anyone was there to greet me, when I spotted a Chinese placard with the usual characters but there was a discernible capital M prefixing the Chinese message. Quite why the person holding the placard didn't approach me since I was probably the only white man in Nanjing at the time, and ostensibly the person holding the card knew he was to greet such a man, simply escaped me. It was the nearest thing to the expected greeting, so I walked towards the placard holder sporting a smile to assure the holder that I wasn't about to berate him, who turned out to be a she, a young girl of late teenage years I guessed. She returned the smile but looked afraid and nervous. Later, I learned that I was the first white

53

man she had ever seen—little wonder that she was a little overwhelmed. She spoke very broken English, but I was impressed by the way she tried hard to make me understand that she was with her father who was waiting back at the car to take them to the factory. Well to call it a car turned out to be something of an exaggeration. It was more like a converted Russian tank, dull camouflage beige in colour, it was constructed from 4mm plate or something near. It would have benefited from shock absorbers or at least springs, and top speed was 35 mph. I took the rear seat with the young girl while father sat next to the driver, who was obviously in his employ. I naturally assumed that the factory was somewhere local to the city and that the totally uncomfortable car could be tolerated for a short journey. Having managed to start the engine, the driver pulled out into the bicycle filled main road. How he managed to miss killing at least two cyclists in doing so intrigued me. The ambient temperature must have registered 35 degrees centigrade, and the humidity and heat inside the car was close to becoming unbearable, although there was bottled water available in the back seat. Even so, I was perspiring profusely although all windows were open, when I raised the question, tongue in cheek to the girl, that the car needed an air conditioning unit. Translating this to her father with some difficulty, I was amazed to hear that the car was indeed fitted with air conditioning, and would I like the driver to switch it on. To achieve this, the car was pulled over to the side of the road and stopped with the engine kept running. Feeling under the dashboard, the driver pulled out two wires with bare ends showing and twisting them together started the A.C. compressor with a terribly loud noise reminiscent of a dog fight emitting from the engine compartment. For a fleeting moment, I imagined I felt cold air, but it was indeed fleeting, for with a bang the dog fight fell silent and that put paid to the air conditioner. I then thought it would be a timely question to ask the girl how long it would take them to reach the factory. I was nonplussed to hear the reply—eight hours. Eight hours in that car—could I last that long? The girl just smiled at the look on my face, but what choice did I have the answer to that was a plain zero. The car wound its way through the suburbs of Nanjing passing gradually poorer neighbourhoods until it ran out of road, replaced by dirt tracks. Every now and then, the sealed road would reappear then disappear again, and for long periods the car would literally be crossing fields and passing through farmyards until I lost complete interest and fell asleep.

I was awakened by loud conversation in Chinese between the father and his driver who was pointing to something in the distance. Looking ahead, I could just make out what looked like the sawn off end of a concrete roadway on high concrete trestles.

It was still daylight, and as we approached the apparition, it materialised itself as a motorway under construction in the middle of nowhere. The two in front were obviously as surprised as I was, which was concerning, and were trying to figure out how to get on to the concrete road, which they were driving alongside but which was fifty feet in the air. By this time, I had realised why the father had purchased a converted Russian tank since no ordinary car would have withstood the rigour of the journey so far, yet unbeknown to me worse was to come. Suddenly, we found ourselves in the middle of a construction site which was 12 inches deep in mud, causing the car to slither around in circles. The surprised construction workers were jumping out of the way of the car which had suddenly appeared in their midst and which refused to stop probably due to mud on the brakes. The car did come to a halt eventually, and the irate workers had strong words with the driver. Things were getting a little hairy until the workers spotted me in the back of the car, when they changed tack and started to push the car towards dry ground, and with their guidance and much effort and shouting, we managed to get the car to the top of a makeshift ramp and on to the motorway. The sight of the seemingly endless concrete ribbon of motorway stretching into the distance lifted my spirits a little, and since we had been travelling some five hours by that time, I conjectured that the concrete would see us to our destination. The driver manoeuvred the car on to the right hand side of the trapezoid shaped eighteen inch high concrete central barrier, and away we went at a rasping 35mph with a decently flat surface beneath us for the first time since leaving the city. There was wilderness on either side of the motorway, and I had no idea where we were and suspected that the driver was similarly handicapped. For sure the finding of the isolated motorway had been unexpected. Certainly, there was no other traffic on the road in either direction. The only distraction which amused me was the occasional signposts in English which read 'Soft Verge', on pole supports stuck in the concrete hard shoulders. Some Chinese construction engineer had obviously been to England to study the motorways, seen the signs and thought 'we'll have some of those.'

I was now wide awake enough to spot in the distance a new concrete bridge crossing the motorway, also remarking to the girl that the bridge arch on their side of the road was impassable, being completely blocked with bamboo scaffolding. This reinforced my suspicion that the motorway was still not commissioned for traffic use, and I had a vision of reaching a sawn off road end still fifty feet in the air— and what if the driver drove off the end in the impending darkness? This vision flashed through my mind and how to convey my fears to the other car occupants. The immediate problem was however how to continue at all, since our path was well and truly blocked by the scaffolding.

Turning around was one option, but that would entail one hour plus drive back, and it was dusk by that time. I joined in the discussion as best I could, and the little girl did her best to get my opinion across to the feuding twosome in the front, when the driver ushered us all out of the car and reversed the vehicle to one side of the road, then revving madly he made a dash for the central barrier. I watched in horror as the car smashed into the concrete trapezoid flipped in the air and landed equally across the blocks and remained balanced, rocking one way then the other. I had never slept under a motorway bridge before, but it was looking like a real possibility. The men tried to heave the vehicle across to the other side, but it was too heavy, and it was then that I realised that I had to take charge, with the two Chinese wringing their hands and the girl near to tears. I gestured the men to follow me and started to dismantle the bamboo scaffolding from under the arch. There was too much to clear it all, but I just wanted the bamboo poles. Using the poles as levers, we three men managed to dump the car off the barrier and on to the other carriageway. That meant of course that we were now driving the wrong way down the motorway in the gradually darkening evening. Not a pleasant experience, especially when after few miles we saw three large construction trucks with headlights blazing spread across the three lanes coming towards us. The truck drivers must have wondered who in the hell would be coming towards them at that time of day on an unfinished motorway, but as we drew near they parted sufficiently to allow us through, waving a greeting as though it was an everyday occurrence. *There must be a way off the motorway*, I thought with some relief. There was! Down another makeshift ramp and into another mud bath and eventually on to a half sealed road with a view in the distance showing the lights of a small town. The girl's father started to jabber and point at the lights, and I got the impression that this was where they were heading. The girl said, "Hotel Hotel" and clapped her hands, and I also felt like clapping but restrained myself.

It was dark as we drove slowly through the shanty town, and I was dismayed at the dilapidated state of the buildings I could barely make out in the dim street lamps. The driver couldn't find the hotel as we drove round and around the shabby streets, and I made a vow to myself that if the hotel was anything like the buildings I could see then I would sleep in the car. Nothing doing! The driver could not find the hotel, when I spotted what I thought to be a taxi. I told the girl to hire the taxi to guide them to the hotel. She jumped out of the car and ran across to the taxi and did just that. Following the taxi, we drove out of the town for about one mile and on turning a sharp right hand bend in the road, there appeared a magnificent huge floodlit hotel which looked brand new. It was unbelievable, the splendour of the place. It was like a glittering palace with tastefully uniformed commissionaire and staff. To me, it was as if someone had waved a magic wand. As we walked into the cavernous foyer, marble floors and pillars all around, large crystal chandeliers down its length, I noticed that we were the only people around except for the numerous staff. The check in desk looked half a mile long and was beautifully made with relief carvings along the lengthy frontage. A check in clerk was positioned every ten feet or so along the desk standing motionless like so many statues in smart hats and uniforms staring straight ahead but no clients except the four, as was confirmed the following morning in the breakfast room, itself the size of a ballroom. The bedrooms were large and opulent, and the facilities throughout were first class. *Maybe there was a city close by*, I thought, because the hotel could in no way be related to the shambles of a town they had just driven through. Apparently, no close by city I was advised, as could be seen next morning. The hotel was literally in the middle of nowhere.

I was feeling much better after a good night's sleep and a western style breakfast, fully ready to meet the challenges of the day—a visit to the owner's premises and a full day writing up my feasibility study, maybe a second or third day producing samples and finalising negotiations. I was certain I could tolerate a few days in that five-star palace.

As we walked to the car park—fortunately ours was the only car on the huge car park, prohibiting comparison with real cars for which I was grateful—I broached the question to the now smiling girl as to the time it would take to reach father's factory. I was shattered to hear eight hours. Another eight hours of god knows what lay in front of us. Had I been in touching distance of civilisation at that moment, I would have definitely absconded. I toyed with the idea of setting fire to the tank conversion—*maybe we could hire a decent car in town*. Then visions of the state of the town ruled out that thought. It should be recorded at this juncture that although I had plenty of cash U.S. Dollars, also Sterling plus an American Express card, none of this was negotiable in China at that time which meant I was effectively broke. This severely restricted my options.

Away we drove down what had been a tarmac road before it crumbled—probably due to the construction traffic when they were building the hotel. I had unwittingly dressed for a day at the office suit, tie, the lot—but soon regretted having done so because the heat and humidity in the car was oppressive, and I quickly shed garments.

Four hours of torture later, we were really in no man's land. No road whatsoever just tracks, wilderness scrub, no farms, and no signs of life. The girl and I had drunk so much bottled water by this time that it was bound to have an effect. I was grateful to hear the girl speak to her father, then to ask me if I would like to use a toilet. It would not have surprised me had there been a toilet in the large boot behind the car, but no. Father said that he would pull in at the next village they came to. Looking at the terrain I thought that could take a while, and so it did—one hour later in fact, by which time I would have settled for a decent bush.

It was like something out of a movie scene, one car driving across barren wasteland as we eventually drove slowly into a small deserted village close by the track.

Through shanty built shelters—they couldn't truthfully be called houses, we stopped on the dusty track passing through what seemed to be the village centre. The four of us stepped out of the car and looked around for someone to hopefully guide us to a toilet when people began ghosting out of the shanties. Before long, there was a crowd of women and children and a sprinkling of old men who closed in around the visitors smiling and gesticulating at me, who although only of average height in European terms felt like a giant amongst the villagers. They touched my clothing and clapped and laughed out loud. The father spoke to them presumably to ask if they had a toilet that we could use, which, looking at the surroundings, was an ambitious request. When the request spread amongst the villagers, they all began to giggle amongst themselves and point in unison towards the scrub surrounding the village, then they began to usher the four travellers in that direction. It quickly became apparent that we were going to have an audience, but not so. In fact, the villagers were pointing towards what appeared to be a stoutly constructed sentry box standing apart from the dwellings with a large black door, and on approach I could see that although narrow it was about three metres long. As the man from space I was allowed to enter first with the villagers encouraging me to go in. The door was heavy and without locks or catches of any kind, and as the door closed behind me, I found myself in pitch darkness. Fortunately, I had a lighter with me, and the glimmer of light showed that the hut was completely empty except for two large four feet high Egyptian like amphora jars with open tops. Not able to figure out what I was supposed do, I quickly relieved myself of the volumes of bottled water in a corner and then using my fingertips managed to open the heavy door and walk out to the cheering crowd of villagers. Having warned the little girl about the heavy door, she went in next but could not get out, and had to be rescued. The father subsequently discovered from the villagers that the toilet was a newly built innovation in the village, and that we were the first ones to try it which was the reason for all the celebration. I did think of giving them a little western know how reference about the large amphora jars but thought better of it. The enthusiastic villagers followed the car to the edge of the village waving madly as the car regained the main dusty dirt track to renew the journey. As we left the confines of the village, the girl turned to me and simply said 'lucky'— to which I started to chuckle assuming that she was referring to the existence of a toilet in such a god forsaken spot. Then she said, "Not toilet—no men." It was only then that I realised that indeed there were no men in the village. The girl replied, "All men gone banditing." They had just christened the toilet in a bandit village.

On and on we drove, occasionally stopping to pour yet another jerry can of petrol into the tank (not metaphorical), only dirt roads and farm tracks to drive along which radically reduced our progress.

By this time, I, who was touching sixty years old at the time, was, although physically fit for my age, feeling the strain of the seemingly endless journey. The car suddenly started to speed along at its near top speed of 35mph. We had reached a narrow but sealed road which ran alongside a high bushy bank to its right side. A sharp right hand turn into a gap in the bank then a steep incline, past a line of two parked cars and two small trucks, and there in front of us was the raging yellow torrent of the Yangtze River. Our driver had driven to the front of a queue, awaiting what, I couldn't guess. There was no jetty, no building or even shanty, just the river— the opposite shore was out of sight, the water looked very menacing, travelling East at rapids speed away to distant Shanghai. I stepped out of the car to see the drivers of the parked vehicles approaching the father and driver with what appeared to be evil intent, their having purloined the front spot. However, when they saw me emerge, they turned around as one and marched back to their own vehicles. Although early evening, it was still sunny daylight and hot and sticky in the high humidity, and I told the girl that I would need to sit in the car.

The car driver swung into the driver's seat and started the engine then attempted to hot wire the AC unit. The two dogs started to fight again which triggered me to try to explain through the girl that the engine would overheat, and the driver should turn off the engine. However, the driver was ecstatic at having conquered the AC unit and smiled broadly at me who was doing my best to get my point across when with a loud bang the car bonnet flew into the air and a water spout shot out of the radiator.

I put my head in my hands, but the car driver assisted by the other drivers in the queue rescued the bonnet and refitted it to the car as though it was an everyday occurrence. Again, I tried to warn them, this time as the men dragged the yellow ochre water from the river edge and poured it into the radiator—they never did find the radiator cap. To my utter amazement, the car engine started first time.

The girl then shouted, "Felly, felly," which puzzled me, until I realised she meant 'ferry.' What puzzled me even more was, where was the ferry? None could be seen. And where would it dock to load? I looked out over the water upstream and down—no signs of any craft whatsoever, and I knew that the ferry would have to be of substantial proportions to accommodate the cars and trucks, and to negotiate the violent waters. The girl said, "Felly come." I was staggered to see emerging from behind a bush overhanging the water, and from downstream, against the current, a large bamboo raft with one man having a ticket machine over his shoulder standing at its centre. There was no sign of any power source attached to the raft, which had old car tyres secured around the periphery, so how was it moving against the current? That anomaly was solved when from behind the overhanging bush emerged the smallest tugboat I had ever seen, which had a large truck tyre fastened to its prow to act as a battering ram and with which the tiny tug bumped the raft upstream. Once in position, the ticket collector cast two ropes on to the shore, and the ferry customers secured them to two stakes onshore. It flashed through my mind that I was in the middle of a Monty Python sketch—but no, the ferry customers had found two wooden car skids in the long grass which they proceeded to bridge the gap from shore to raft. I stood open mouthed watching, barely believing what I was seeing, and said to the girl that there was no way I was going to get in the car to be driven on to the raft.

She replied saying that if I preferred I could walk on to the raft and stand with the ticket collector, who by now was issuing tickets from his ancient ting-ting ticket machine to the five drivers. I could not envision how the raft I was looking at could accommodate two small trucks, two cars and one converted Russian tank— there simply wasn't the space. The ferryman had to leave one car behind, but how they got the rest of the vehicles on to the raft defied belief.

The raft was constantly rocking in the swell of the onrushing water, and I watched from the safety of the shore as the tiny tug's large tyre kept the raft in position while loading took place.

Only myself and the ferryman now stood onshore, and the latter was urging me to board the raft before he removed the car skids. Against my better judgement, I did so having little choice in the matter and reasoning that if the Chinese could do it, then so could I—but I was far from happy and stood in between the vehicles which seemed the safest of a very unsafe situation. Never will I forget that trip across the Yangtze. The fast moving waters threatened to sweep the raft downstream, but I was absolutely amazed at the incredible skill of the tug boat helmsman on who my life depended as he bumped and pushed the raft across the river moving his little boat from one end of the raft to the other. Wet up to my waist, I was grateful to see the opposite shoreline approach, which we eventually reached, but the sight of a car vertical on its nose in the water close to shore did nothing for my confidence. I was first to leap onshore and watched as the vehicles unloaded. I wondered how long it would have taken to train the ferryman and tug boat crew to perfect the performance I had just witnessed and how many lives were lost in the doing.

If I thought that that part of the journey was done and dusted, I was dismayed to find that for some reason I could not immediately fathom the security guards at the barrier to the ferry terminal, or shed would be more apt, would not let us drive through. There developed a raucous argument between the father and the guards. All the other vehicles were allowed through. It transpired that our car driver had lost the ferry ticket, worth about a US nickel, which he was obliged to hand to the guards before being allowed through. The row was getting out of hand, and even my presence at the barrier couldn't quell the shouting. It was then that I noticed that the guards were in fact soldiers complete with weapons. The father offered them money which made matters worse, when I, by now at the end of my tether, began to intercede with the soldiers telling them in English how stupid they were to think that the party could have arrived from anywhere else other than the ferry, which was only yards from the barrier, from which the guards had witnessed them drive off the raft. That did the trick, and to the surprise of the girl and her father, the barrier was lifted. By this time, I had reconciled myself to be immune to whatever further surprises lay ahead, after all I was a seasoned world traveller by that time and felt myself to be prepared for almost any occurrence. I would be wrong in that assumption.

We drove into Jiujiang, which was our destination, in an almost stately manner, with beaming smiles on the faces of my fellow passengers, and respectful, probably grateful clapping from the young girl. "Home, home," she said almost in tears. She later confirmed to me that that was her very first trip away from her home, and it then occurred to me that she probably had held the same reservations that he had felt along the way—that they never would arrive. Jiujiang turned out to be an enchanting place, surrounded by the kind of gherkin shaped huge mounds or hills covered in whispery foliage and unusual flowering trees and bushes—as seen on Chinese paintings and pottery. The town itself with a beautiful lake at its centre was truly scenic in its hilly setting, and I was impressed at the sight as they pulled to a halt at the entrance door to an obviously grand hotel in its day but which was badly in need of a facelift. Huge pillars adorned the frontage and it reminded me of a neglected English folly, but a huge one at that. The father who was a genuine sort of chap was anxious that I would be pleased with the hotel and began to describe the history of the place via his daughter. Apparently, the hotel was a favourite of Chairman Mao no less, who holidayed regularly there with his entourage. I thought that if it was fine by Chairman Mao then it should be acceptable to myself, and together we walked to the reception desk. The inside was even in greater need of refurbishment than the outside but had obviously been splendid in its day—gold leaf everywhere, large expensive looking curtains draped across windows which hadn't been cleaned since Mao passed away, marble floors and statues all around, but none depicting the Chairman himself which I would have expected following the prologue outside. Or maybe not so surprising. The room shown to me was large indeed, and sparsely furnished, but the bed was big enough for three or four occupants, and the bedding was clean and good quality. The attached bathroom was again large with quaint toilets, yes there were two, two of everything in fact—no showers but baths you could bath an elephant in. No soaps but plenty of stiff brushes in sinks and baths. I felt I could make do, reminding myself of where I was and what I could reasonably expect. The big let-down was the hotel food. Atrocious would be an understatement. Having been accustomed to enjoying wonderful far eastern cuisine, I expected better, but after the first evening meal and morning breakfast, I felt obliged to complain to the hotel manager, who though not speaking any English, did get the message through sign language. The outcome was that I would be allowed to go into the hotel kitchen and cook my own food, which I did during my one-week stay. I drew the line though at plucking my own chickens. The restaurant food in the town was very good, and I would eat out regularly with the father along to pay the bill since I could not use my foreign money. The only problem with eating out was the fact that I would be surrounded at our table by curious children from the streets laughing and asking for titbits. Not urchins, just well cared for kids to who I was something of a curiosity and a celebrity combined.

I arrived at the factory site on the first morning to find a delegation comprising the town's grandees awaiting our arrival. There was the 'Mayor' together with several prominent business tycoons in their ludicrously shiny suits, a small intelligent looking individual dressed in shabby khaki attire taking notes, *but no cameras in sight so it's probably not the press*, I thought. Having shaken hands and bowed to everyone I listened while the father addressed the throng, obviously gaining credence for having attracted the farang all the way from England to his humble factory.

Still it was all in good humour, and I smiled along with everyone else. More hand shaking ensued as the dignitaries bade their goodbyes, and it was time for me to begin my assessment and potential of the establishment.

I was now becoming popular with the kitchen staff at the hotel, who became fascinated with the dishes I was creating for myself involving the only ingredients available— plucked chicken, peculiar vegetables, duck eggs and potatoes and rice of course. I held no illusions that I could cook, but needs must, and though I was a virgin cook, I tried to remember what my wife did when at home. I didn't starve but would not recommend my creations to anyone.

On the third day of my stay, the father asked if I would like a guided tour of the town. We had been working long hours and a break was in order, so I accepted the father's offer, on condition that he would bring his daughter along to interpret, to which he agreed. It was indeed a very old and fascinating town, boasting a famous multi-tiered teahouse and a one thousand plus years old monastery which was creepy and very absorbing to me. Every artefact in the place looked priceless, the statues, the pottery vases, some of which were huge. Lit by candles alone it had low ceilings and was very dark. Suddenly from behind a roughly hewn pillar ghosted a small slight figure shrouded from head to foot in a black cloak who confronted me causing me to pull up short to avoid a collision. The figure was slight of stature and much less than five feet tall. Two bony arms appeared from under the cloak and drew aside the face veil to reveal a pale and serene almost childlike Chinese ladies' face, with blue eyes and a welcoming smile, carrying a lit candle, which she held up to my face.

She began to talk in Chinese to me in a high pitched voice looking me straight in the eye, while maintaining a beaming smile the whole time. She was a nun as translated to me by the girl, and she was welcoming me to her sanctity within the monastery, also saying I was blessed with goodness and good health. She had never met a westerner before, but she had heard good things about them and was pleased that I had honoured her monastery with my visit. Then she inserted one hand beneath her robe and withdrew it, holding a shiny red apple which she offered to me saying that if I ate the blessed apple I would live a long and healthy life. I accepted the apple and thanked the nun for her gift, then promised to eat it when I was back at the hotel. In truth, I wanted to wash the apple beforehand. The little figure then closed up her veil and scurried behind the column she had emerged from. I could have spent much more time in the monastery since the whole place intrigued me, but we departed following the meeting with the tiny nun.

We lunched at a semi-open-air café, again myself being the attraction for the locals, who stood in a small crowd at a distance watching me eat my meal, with the children running up to the table to get a good look. As we left the café, I thought I saw in the distance a church spire, which was the last thing I expected to see in the still communist dominated country, in which the red guards had some time ago burned and looted everything of Christian significance or indeed anything of any religious connotation. The girl confirmed that it was indeed a church spire, and would I like to see the church. Having been raised and schooled as a Catholic, I felt the need to have a look at what was left of what I thought would be a previous missionary settlement of some kind. As we approached the small but well-constructed stone built church, reminiscent of the village churches in the U.K, I could see that the building was undamaged including the stained glass windows which surprised me. Within the church there was nothing but plain walls, no altar, no religious artefacts or pictures, no pews—nothing at all. We were greeted at the entrance door by a Chinese family of some eight or nine people, who turned out to be the custodians of the church, and who lived on the premises. The family had been custodians of the church in its heyday, and a succession of the family had taken it upon themselves to look after the building despite beatings and loss of life to the red guards during the purge, and they

66

vowed to stay there until the return of 'the holy people' to restart the 'learning.' The church and surrounding premises were spotlessly clean, and the family were overjoyed and in tears to meet me which they said was a signal for the start of the new beginning they had been praying for over many years. I felt humbled at their dedication and shook the hands of every member of the family to whom I expressed the hope that my unannounced visit had given them renewed confidence.

Two days before, I was due to leave for home, I expressed to the father that there was no way I would be returning to Hong Kong by the car route I had endured in coming, and that the father must somehow arrange a flight to get me back. The father said that the only airport reachable was a military airport nearby which did not take commercial passengers, but that he would contact the local military hierarchy to see what could be done as an alternative. The following day, I was told that by using his contact with the mayor and cronies they had between them 'persuaded' the military commander to get me on a military flight which was a special flight from some far flung place which was just happening to call in at Jiujiang to collect some soldiers. The only snag was that the plane was not flying to Hong Kong, but to a military airport some 200 miles North of Shenzhen from where Kowloon and eventually Hong Kong can be reached by monorail. How much Yuan this arrangement cost the father I never knew, but I did know that such arrangements were possible in China at that time. I was nevertheless relieved to hear that I was at least to fly most of the way back. On my arrival at the military airport North of Shenzhen, I was to be collected by car which would drive up from Hong Kong to convey me back to my Hong Kong hotel. *Perfect*, I thought. I was also told specifically that on my arrival at the military airport I should on no account board either of the two Mercedes buses which were to take the passengers into whatever town was closest, otherwise I would be stranded. To wait for the car from Hong Kong was imperative to my safety. I listened carefully to the instructions since I realised that I really would be in trouble without the girl to translate and having a wallet full of currency I could not use.

The evening before the final day of my stay at the hotel, I hosted the father and daughter to dinner which I myself had prepared in the hotel kitchen to the delight of the hotel chefs to whom I had become something of a celebrity, using the pigeon English I had taught them which raised many a laugh.

I was anxious for the father to agree with the hotel manager and himself how the hotel bill would be settled at checkout the following day. The job had gone well, and everyone was well pleased with the progress made, and despite the tribulations, I had enjoyed visiting Jiujiang and meeting with the Chinese people who had gone out of their way to make me welcome. The father and I went to the reception desk to settle the payment arrangement to be made by me on my checkout the following day. I offered to pay the bill out of my travel money if only the manager would accept the currency I had. The manager looked at my American Express card and retired with it to the back office obviously to take advice from his bank. On returning, he agreed that the card was valid and could be used to check me out, to the obvious relief of the father who must have spent at least in local terms, a considerable sum arranging the flight I had requested.

Having said goodbye to my fellow chefs, myself and hosts assembled at the checkout desk at 4:45pm in time to reach the airport by 5:30pm to catch the scheduled 6:00pm flight as instructed. Disaster struck when the now different hotel manager refused to accept the credit card saying it was worthless in China and advising me to go to the local Bank of China branch to ask their advice but to leave my luggage behind. The father became exasperated having already supposedly received clearance on the card, and a confrontation ensued, but to no avail. The bank closed at 5:00pm, it was then three minutes to five, and a dash was made to the car to attempt to reach the bank in time. It was closed, and the three men began banging furiously on the formidably constructed front door in an attempt to raise someone but without success. As we were about to accede to despair and frustration, a small door cut into a large double yard door situated next to the bank opened, and a lady's head peeked out. It was the bank manager who was holding an afterhours training session for her staff. Restraining myself from kissing her on the cheek, we explained the unfortunate situation to the lady, who promptly unlocked the heavy bank door and let them in.

The bank manager confirmed that the American Express card was not negotiable in China, and that the only way to pay the bill was by cash, at which point I showed my sterling and dollars to the lady who did a quick calculation on her abacus and arrived at an exchange rate and bank fee. Yuan was counted out to meet the bill only to find that the bank did not have enough Yuan to meet the bill, and the bank vault was on time lock. The bank lady was obviously distressed at not being able to help us out of the situation and probably broke all the rules of banking and national security by telling us where the nearest black market foreign exchange dealer was holed up. To make up the shortfall we had to find him quick since time was running out. Holed up he was as well, down a seedy narrow side street in a wooden shanty, dirty and untidy, he was most suspicious of our arrival, thinking it was a raid. I was unsure of what the father said to him, and suspected that he used the bank manager's recommendation of him, but something caused him to calm down and provide enough Yuan, although at an inflated exchange rate, to make up the difference. Now running was too slow, and we sprinted back to the car and returned to the hotel where we covered the reception desk with the voluminous Yuan bank notes which took the manager what seemed like an age to count. Released at last, I glanced at my watch which showed 5:30pm. Would we make the airport in time? The driver drove at his top speed of 35 mph out of town and reached the military airport at 5:50pm where we were stopped at the barrier by soldier guards with weapons.

My presence seemed to upset the guards, and they gabbled between themselves and used the guardhouse phone before lifting the barrier to let them through. At the check in table, for that is what it was, in a very primitive Nissan hut, the soldiers refused to allow the father and daughter through to the departure area since they were not travelling. However, the little girl was not having that, and she berated the soldiers into letting her accompany me into the departure lounge which was really the far end of the same Nissan hut. Seated on wooden benches along the sides of the lounge were the other passengers.

One or two civilians, but mostly soldiers, they stared at me incessantly—probably the first white man to fly from that airport. To her credit, the girl would not leave my side, and she spoke sharply to the other passengers who were making me feel a little uneasy. It was then announced that the plane was delayed by 35 minutes, and this proved to be correct. Before boarding, I thanked the daughter for her diligence in assisting me on the trip, without which I would have struggled to complete my task.

The plane was a fifty seat made in China—a twin engine turbo prop in army camouflage carrying mostly soldiers but with five or six civilians already aboard, I took my seat beside one of the soldiers. Where was it taking me? I had no idea, but I had the car and driver sent from Hong Kong to collect me for reassurance that I would be safe. The flight lasted one and a half hours before the plane landed in drizzling rain on another military airfield in a remote area of the countryside. One landing strip and one small Nissan hut contrived the sum total of the airport surrounded by a high wire mesh fence and a barrier entrance. As informed to me, two single deck Mercedes buses were parked adjacent to the hut. All passengers disembarked from the plane and including the crew and ground staff from the hut all boarded the two buses—but no car from Hong Kong. I stood alone in the rain and gloom clutching my two suitcases, and for the first time in my much travelled career, I felt real apprehension and vulnerability. No one approached me though I tried to speak with the civilian ground staff and the plane crew, no one spoke English, and everyone completely ignored me. I was stranded in the middle of nowhere in the semi darkness and drizzling rain. The buses were filled, and everyone was aboard except me, who had been warned not to get on the buses otherwise I would be in trouble. As the buses started to move towards the opened barrier with not another soul around, I felt I had to do something, so I dropped my suitcases and ran to the barrier which I lowered to stop the first bus from leaving. Jumping on to the bus, I called down the bus aisle, "Does anyone speak English?" but all I got was blank stares. I then raised the barrier to allow the bus through, then lowered it again to stop the second bus. "Does anyone speak

English?" This time a small hand was raised at the far back of the bus. I beckoned the hand to come forward and out stepped a small civilian man who left the bus to join me. When the Chinese man started to speak, I could not believe how well he spoke English, virtually with no accent at all. It transpired that the man was a Hong Kong business man who had travelled into China seeking contacts, furthermore, he had been educated at Manchester College of Technology which was my hometown. It was at that moment that I realised I had met my guardian angel. In the remote middle of China on a remote military airfield in the drizzling rain and darkness, and despite the isolation of China to the outside world at that time, to meet such a person it couldn't be anyone else. Steven Pu listened while I related my predicament then advised me to stay close to him because we were in serious bandit territory, where one false move such as hiring a taxi could well result in being kidnapped, driven into the countryside to be robbed and even killed, so lawless was the place. Not that there were any taxis around to hire in that desolate spot. I then opened the barrier and jumped on to the bus to bewildered stares from the other passengers, dragging my heavy suitcases behind, I managed to stand in the aisle alongside Steven who was seated. The bus trundled out of the airport compound, but not on to a road for there was no road, just a field then another field, then yet another, which caused the bus to sway to the undulations of the uneven surface throwing me one way then the other until finally, the bus reached a dirt road, then finally a narrow sealed road which took them into a small town. The streetlights barely glowed in the darkness until the bus came to a halt in the town centre, a square with brightly lit shops and restaurants around the periphery. All passengers alighted and went on their way, but I stayed close to Steven who suggested that they eat in one of the many restaurants, to which I replied that the money I had in plenty was not negotiable. Steven then told me that he would fund all expenses in getting us back to Hong Kong to which I had no option but to agree on the understanding that Steven would be recompensed in full on reaching Hong Kong. Steven however said that he would not accept any recompense because England had given him his education, and he was only too pleased to be able to repay a

71

little in kind. No amount of protestation by me would change his mind. On enquiring Steven as to the mode of transport they would be taking to reach Hong Kong, I was staggered to hear that it would be by taxi, and a seven hour journey at that. We had a good quality meal in a nearby restaurant, then Steven went to the local taxi rank closely followed by myself so as not to lose him, since it had long ago dawned on me that without Steven my situation would become dire indeed.

I couldn't imagine being able to hire a taxi from a small town taxi rank to go on a fourteen hour return journey in the darkness, and I certainly couldn't imagine what it would cost. Nevertheless, following some serious haggling and not a little shouting with the other taxi drivers joining in, Steven struck a bargain and the best car in the rank was chosen by all the taxi drivers which was not saying much since they were all twenty years old or more and small four seaters. Could the two of them get their luggage in apart from any other concerns? This thought crossed my mind. We did, but there was barely enough room for the two of them in the rear seat, and the car was well down on its suspension. The sound of the engine told me that they would be lucky to get out of town never mind distant Hong Kong. Not having any other options of getting to their destination, i.e. no direct trains civil air flights or buses, we could only sit tight and hope. It was 10pm and pitch dark as they left the confines of the town on pot holed roads, and we two weary passengers tried to get some sleep, trusting that the taxi driver didn't follow suit as they motored for hours until the car stopped due to a line of truck traffic. The driver eventually got out of the car to enquire the reason for the lengthy hold up, only to return to the car with the news that there was a multi vehicle collision ahead of them, and they would have to take a diversion. What the driver didn't tell Steven was that the diversion would put a further hour or more on their journey, and that there would be no sealed roads to drive on. For the next four hours, the car skidded its way on muddy tracks and across fields and farmland, how it didn't bog down entirely baffled me, who had formed the opinion that the driver was navigating his way by compass. The tortuous drive eventually brought us into sight of a town, but I was elated and cheered by the view beyond the town showing the neon skyline of Shenzhen— never had a sight been so welcome to my eyes—civilization at last.

The car, now covered in mud, came to a halt at the monorail terminus which connects Shenzhen to Hong Kong, and Steven paid the taxi driver his dues plus something extra which he richly deserved for staying awake if nothing else. Steven purchased two first-class rail tickets, and I said a silent thank you for my delivery as we entered the colony and hired a taxi to my hotel from the rail terminus. I again tried to recompense Steven but to no avail, then thanked him profusely for his generosity and protection in what had been a white knuckle situation and which for me could well have had dire consequences in retrospect. I did, however, send a letter of thanks to Steven's Hong Kong address. I later learned that the promised car had in fact been sent by Lawrence Li and had arrived at the remote military airfield, but due to the arrival delay and the threat to the driver of physical violence by the military ground staff, the frightened driver had scurried back to Hong Kong leaving me in the lurch. A worried Lawrence had in fact alerted the authorities of my precarious predicament, but thanks to the chance meeting with my guardian angel, all was well that ended well. I turned down Lawrence's generous terms for me to take on the assignment due to the fact that it would not have been safe to take my family along to darkest China at that time and that would have been my stipulation to take the contract.

Nevertheless, I was grateful for having had the opportunity to meet and assist the local hard working people whose only ambition at the time was to improve their lot in life through sheer persistence and effort, despite the severely restrictive regime they were subject to. I did contract the assignment to a third party, and the factory was completed and commissioned eventually.

Chapter Ten
The 23-Inch Seam (1959)

I had only two weeks to go to the completion of my nine months practical work experience which had entailed working alongside the coal miners at the coalface. Truth be known, I had barely survived the 6:00am starts and 3:00pm finish, five days a week working in horrendous and dangerous conditions, particularly since my ambition on leaving grammar school had been to become a journalist, but military conscription had put paid to that. To escape that two year compulsory commitment thus to be able to continue my e d u c a t i o n, I was forced to work in an 'essential' industry which in my locale meant coal mining. The year was 1951, and the post war economy was still in recovery mode in which coal was the energy king. The NCB management course I was on was open to the likes of myself and university post graduates. Most of the latter group fled the scene when subjected to the compulsory nine months underground preliminary work experience, which was little wonder due to the terrible working conditions and back breaking work coupled with the obvious dangers.

The seasoned and uncompromising miners responsible for my training knew that I had only two weeks training left and therefore arranged for me to spend the remaining time working with a 'special' group of miners which I was not aware of.

I had been accustomed to working on three and one half to four feet high coal faces tough though that was, but I was now assigned to this 'special' group as a parting shot to test my 'bottle', but I was not privy to this reasoning, and no one told me of the conditions I was heading for on that morning. I thought it strange when walking along the main nine feet high tunnel with the group that the foreman had halted them then proceeded to call out numbers. The miners formed a single line, and each was handed a miners shovel. I was placed halfway along the single file, wondering what was going on up front, as they continued their march onwards.

Suddenly, the men in front of me seemed to be disappearing into the right hand side of the tunnel. On reaching the front of the line, I was surprised to see a hole cut half way up the wall measuring twenty three inches high and forty eight inches wide from which emerged the delivery end of a conveyor belt running flat along the floor of the hole, that is void of conveyor rollers or structure of any kind—there was no room to install such niceties. "Up you go," came a voice from behind, and I felt a push in the small of my back. Too late to ask questions now. I wasn't the biggest fellow but could barely crawl along the miniature tunnel let alone hurry up, and my helmet was scraping the roof as I tried my best to keep moving along. With only my helmet light to see by, it was like crawling into hell and the butterflies in my stomach were sending out panic signals. Of the twenty miners in the tunnel I had ten on either side of me as I shone my headlight on to the reflective high quality twenty three inch high coal seam squashed between the limestone roof and floor of the tunnel. Short round wooden prop supports ran in a line behind me looking totally inadequate for the purpose, and the void behind the prop line known as the 'gob' stretched away for some fifty yards or so into the darkness awaiting the controlled roof fall to close roof on to floor. Before I had time to allow the conditions to influence my composure, a piercing whistle rang out, and the conveyor belt started to run along the floor behind me. The previous night work shift had set their explosive shots which had broken the front face of the seam into large lumps some of which could be shovelled along the floor and on to the conveyor behind the miners. The larger lumps however were moved on to the conveyor by the men hooking their legs behind them and dragging them along the floor until the belt took them away. I was shown the methodology and did my best to emulate the experienced miners but was no match. After two hours of this, I had had enough, but there was four hours to go excluding lunch break before I would be able to get out of the tunnel, for no way could I get past the men working downstream of me.

Going to the canteen for lunch was not an option, but work was temporarily suspended at the sound of the piercing whistle to enable the miners to eat their sandwiches and drink their flask tea, that is if it had survived the morning's hectic goings on. Some men put their snap tin and flask into the highly dangerous 'gob' to escape the flying coal and shovels. It was risky but ensured you preserved your lunch. Coal dust, particularly from high quality coal, gives your sandwich a crunchy texture, but it doesn't taste half bad. During the lunch break, the miners explained to me what to do in the event of a 'weight' occurring. This phenomenon, which I was assured did not occur often, was the name given to an incident whereby the roof of the tunnel would descend slowly to the floor for no particular reason. This was the reason that wooden props were used in favour of the steel supports used in thicker seams. When the wooden props began to feel the excessive pressure of the descending roof, they would squeal, and the noise would warn the miners to vacate immediately and scramble to get out quickly. My spirits were not exactly raised by this disclosure, and had I been told of this prior, I doubted that I would have agreed to the experience. Still, I considered my chances of getting out were at best ten to one and not twenty to one as could have been the case. At the end of the shift, indicated once more by the piercing whistle, the conveyor stopped, and one by one, the men dropped out of the tunnel end, but it took a deal of effort from me to crawl the distance, being prodded on by the miners behind me in no uncertain terms. Once out and standing in the seemingly cavernous main tunnel, but which was itself only some nine feet high, the foreman pointed out to me a miners' helmet which was hung on a nail on the wall just above the 23inch seam entrance which I had not noticed on my way in on that morning. It belonged to the last man to emerge from the seam after the last 'weight' one month previous whose helmet had been removed from his head by the descending roof. The helmet was bent double upon itself, a testimony to anyone entering the twenty three inch seam to beware and to listen out for the squealing props. The miners did shake my hand before dispersing knowing that it had been quite an ordeal for me, but as a parting shot assured me, tongue in cheek, that it took a real man to do it twice. I did it again the following day, but twice was enough.

Chapter Eleven
The Way to Olampi (1972)

I had been working long hours including most weekends, and fatigue was showing on my countenance according to my wife. Unknown to me, she had been secretly conspiring with two of her closest counterparts on the island to plan a trip to get me away and unwind my tension. There were many captivating places they could visit on Taiwan Island, its pre China name of Formosa meaning beautiful island, being no misnomer. Announcing her final hatching to me, who had no idea there was a plot afoot, it was, that together with two good friends from the diplomatic office they would allow me to drive them 250 miles or so to the most southern tip of the island and the seaside resort of Olampi for a few days relaxation on the beach. Needless to say, I was not enamoured with the idea of slogging my way that distance just to unwind and suggested a couple of strong manhattans as an alternative plan. However, the cat was out of the bag amongst the ladies mafia, and before long, two other couples had asked if they could tag along in their car. The two extras quickly became four then six then ten, and soon it became apparent that I would be leading a car caravan down the island. Things got out of hand to the point that a site meeting was held amongst the ladies chaired by the wife of an American army captain—the Vietnam War was being waged at the time, and I suggested that maybe they could organise a landing craft assault on Olampi from the sea. Not to be deterred, and by employing the well-known American flair for organising people from other countries, it was finally announced that using his influence, the captain would provide a fifty seat luxury air conditioned coach from the U.S. barracks, with driver, to take the multi-national multitude on the trip. Furthermore, the US army would arrange for two stops en route at their two military depots and provide snack meals at their expense for the weary travellers. Things were looking up I thought, maybe it could prove beneficial after all—at least it nullified the idea of me having to drive the distance, and I agreed to take the necessary days from work. Objective achieved, my wife was more than happy and organised the children's school break accordingly. The subtropical sun at Olampi would be most uplifting, especially since Taipei being in the temperate zone was cool and rainy at that time. Then, the US army, to everyone's surprise, offered free accommodation to the trippers at their barrack huts located in Olampi, including the use of their canteen. Things were really looking up, and the organising ladies were well pleased with themselves—three cheers for the US military.

The instructions were to gather in front of Suzie's kitchen shop in Tienmu at 6:00am sharp on the day to board the coach and go from there. I was there early to drop our luggage and wife and children then to search for a safe parking spot for my car. Soon the rest of the passengers began to arrive, mostly American families with teenagers who brought along masses of equipment including surfboards, skateboards, backpacks and all manner of miscellaneous paraphernalia. The nations represented were 70% US to 30% European, but on the day, all were as one in that we looked forward to the trip—but where was the promised coach? After one hour's wait during which time people were getting fidgety in the increasingly humid conditions, telephone calls were made from the local shop, which itself was doing a roaring trade amongst the teenagers particularly, with snacks and drinks. The American chairlady cum chief organiser was becoming increasingly wound up on the phone in trying to find out what had happened to the coach, when down the street coming towards the crowd appeared a basic yellow American school bus. Slatted wood seats, no air conditioning, complete with Chinese school bus driver. No explanation was given as to why the air conditioned luxury coach had been substituted, but the youngsters didn't seem fazed at all and proceeded to fill the bus with all their clutter, but it was apparent to me at that moment that it was going to be a most uncomfortable twelve hour ride down the island. That turned out to be the understatement of the day.

It was difficult to find even standing room given the vast amount of seagoing boards inflated porpoises, ducks, beach umbrellas, and folding chairs which the Americans found indispensable to their trip despite pleas from the more reserved European passengers to dump some of the paraphernalia. Seats were found for the more senior travellers, with the teenagers standing in the aisle clutching their stuff. Not to forget the beer—we can't leave the beer, American beer from the PX duty free, ten crates of it. The lot would be consumed during the trip, most of it by two or three beer connoisseurs. Onwards down Chung Shan North road then South on to the road known locally as suicide run, driving at a steady 35 mph towards Chungli. To drive a car down that stretch of road in those days was a life threatening journey, which I had experienced first-hand on many occasions when it was not unusual to pass the bodies of road accident victims laying on the roadside en route. The major hazard was the many speeding pig trucks—open backed lorries housing a two tier wire mesh enclosure crammed tight with squealing pigs off to slaughter. The reason for the high speed was the rush to get the pigs to the slaughter house since the drivers were paid according to the weight of the animals on delivery. That is, the loss of weight incurred by perspiration during transit, which was considerable in the often hot climate, was deducted from their wages. They were madmen drivers with no regard for other drivers on the road who would give them a wide berth at all times. They often could be seen stopped in the middle of the road running to and from the paddy fields carrying water to throw over the steaming hot pigs to cool them down. The numerous scooter and motorbike drivers were fodder for these crazy pig trucks

The bus was nearing Taichung, a quarter way down the island, and the wooden seat slats had long since etched themselves firmly across everyone's backside when the madam of ceremonies announced that the US barracks there would be their first stop for refreshment and toilet breaks. The bus was stopped for security checks at the barrier where the guard climbed on to the bus and told the throng that the barracks was closed for painting and renovation of the canteen. On hearing this, the numerous people needing the toilet all shouted to the guard to let them in to at least relieve themselves, led by the three connoisseurs. The guard shouted back that he had no authority to allow that and had been told to let no one through the gate. The US captain then stepped out of the bus and began to pull rank on the two squaddies manning the gate. Telephone calls later between gate and base commander, the barrier was raised, and the trippers were allowed off the bus. The commander emerged from his office to see what all the commotion was about and apologised to the crowd saying that he had not been advised of their arrival, and that the base was indeed closed for painting, also that he would provide toilet facility but could only offer bottled water as a refreshment, which he did.

Back on the road, the crowded bus weaved its way through Taichung suburbs to reach the road South beyond.

The captain's wife announced that the next stop would be at Tainan, some two thirds way to their destination, where they would be treated to free refreshment and a chance to relax a little before the last leg of the journey to Olampi. By now, it came as no surprise to me to find that the US Barracks at Tainan was also closed for painting—it seemed they had maybe ventured to go to Olampi on US national canteen painting day, and the embarrassment expressed by the captain's wife culminated in the whole bus erupting in protracted good natured laughter, in which everyone joined in—including the captain and his wife. I then stood and on behalf of the European contingent assured the company that they had surmounted their bad luck for the day and that things could only get better to celebrate his break to unwind.

Fourteen hours had passed when the bus entered the outskirts of Olampi in total darkness. No one including the Chinese driver had any idea of the direction to take them to the US army base, and they meandered the dark streets with two of the beer connoisseurs—one Englishman and one American—hanging their heads and shoulders from the bus access steps searching for someone to direct them. Although the time showed 9pm, the streets were deserted. Around and around they drove through the narrow streets of the town, and most of the travellers were nodding in their seats or draped across their surf boards using the inflatables as pillows. Finally, came a shout from one of the lookouts who had spotted an individual walking the streets, whereby he jumped from the bus to catch up with him and the bus stopped. As it did so, a few of the men who were still awake, including myself, made their way through the packed bus aisle to alight from the bus to lend a hand. The poor local turned to see a small posse of men walking towards him, took fright and fled. Thwarted, the men stopped to look around, then spotted a substantial wood-built archway directly in front of the bus outlined in the headlights. The roadway being much too narrow to turn around the only way was forward. The archway was some 50 yards through in depth—tunnel-like—and the width of the narrow road. The captain waved the bus forward, and there was no doubting that the arch was tall enough to allow passage in. Slowly, the bus moved forward with the men walking backwards in front waving it on. Suddenly I, using my engineer's eyes, realised that the tunnel roof was sloping downwards, and the bus was not going to make it. I called a warning to the driver and the other men, but they kept waving it forwards, being bleary eyed and a little tipsy. I shouted repeatedly to stop the bus, but it was too late. With a horrible scraping sound, the bus jammed itself firmly under the arched roof. The noise disturbed the clients of a small drinking bar just beyond the arch and the Chinese drinkers ran to investigate. At least they now had sufficient manpower, and together with the men from the bus, they tried to push the bus backwards, but to no avail—it was well and truly jammed tight. Just then, a police siren screamed out, and two squad cars appeared in front of the bus—someone from the bar must have alerted them. The police were ready to arrest everyone present until the US captain found the chief, who spoke sufficient English to make him aware that the American military were in charge of the bus, at which point the police inspector calmed down and became suddenly cooperative. He also knew the way to the barracks. Whereupon, the police and the local drinkers all had a good laugh at the predicament of the invaders, giving little thought to what damage had been done to their archway. Laughter turned to incredulity when the police attached tow ropes from their small SUVs to the front of the bus and began to pull the bus through the archway. With loud screeching and wailing, the bus was lifting the whole wooden archway off its foundations without regard for whatever could be above it, severely denting the top of the bus as it did so. The people still inside covered their ears against the crunching noise until the battered school bus finally emerged from the archway, leaving a trail of broken timber behind it.

The bus followed the police cars to the police station where a full transcript of the incident was entered into the daybook and countersigned by the captain. What compensation if any was claimed against the US military was never made public.

On arrival at the military barracks, the captain together with myself and the American connoisseur together with the police chief who had guided them, went to the check in point. It was midnight by this time, but luckily, there was a Chinese custodian standing behind a narrow ticket office like desk with just his head and shoulders visible above it. The police chief did the talking in Chinese but judging by the animated discussion with the check in clerk, things were not going well. Little wonder since the chief announced to the travellers' contingent that the Chinese army had commandeered the barracks for their annual 'Generals rest and recuperation weekend' and that all the accommodation was filled with military and local dignitaries. On hearing this, the American connoisseur reached over the high office counter and grabbing the custodian by the lapels physically dragged him over into the foyer.

The frightened man was rescued by the others present, and he ran away down the corridor shouting Chinese expletives as he went. The police chief then advised the party that their best bet was to follow his car to a five star hotel complex way up in the hills which overlooked Olampi to seek accommodation for the night and review the situation next morning. It was an 'any port in a storm' situation, and they had little choice but to comply. They bade farewell to the chief on reaching the complex and thanked him for his genuine concern and assistance. The hotel car park was now overflowing with travel weary passengers, and though the youngsters were still ebullient, the older sect were almost out on their feet, some needing assistance to climb the many steps leading to the entrance doors. It was quite a splendid place, but true to form, they only had four double rooms vacant, then following desperation talks with the Chinese management, they finally allowed the rest of the crowd to bed down in the foyer or any corner they could find, even on the sweeping thick carpeted stair case to the first floor. Furthermore, they opened up their restaurant though it was well into the small hours, and their skeleton kitchen night staff provided drinks and basic rice based snacks. Full marks to the management of the hotel who only charged for the four rooms. Family and I spent the night in one of the hotel corridors as did many others, and the other paying guests couldn't believe their eyes when they emerged from their rooms the following morning to find bedraggled refugees strewn all over the place.

Word reached the hotel by courier the following morning that for whatever reason, the US army barracks in the town had been vacated by the Chinese and was available for occupancy. However, the merrymakers had had enough, and all booked into the hotel for the second night of their stay, including the captain and his wife. To round off a truly memorable stress breaker, the heavens opened on that morning, out of season monsoon rains which trapped everyone in the hotel until 3:00pm when the sun appeared and everyone rushed to the tropical beach using the battered bus. The sun shone for no more than two hours before the rains returned, but that was sufficient time for several children to become badly sunburnt. Prior to the beach trip, the ad hoc committee had gained approval to set out for Taipei at 6 : 0 0 pm that evening to travel overnight against minimal traffic and without stops at the two military bases en route, who would probably be allowing their paint to dry anyway. With roadside rest stops and midnight re-fuelling, the bus trundled into Taipei at 8 : 0 0 am the following morning, looking like it had just returned from the Vietnam conflict. Much of the teenagers' stuff had been abandoned en route making sleeping in the bus aisle somewhat easier for them. Strangely on disembarking in Tienmu, everyone was unfazed by the traumatic trip—no one was laughing—but remained friends, which was in itself amazing and stranger still the experience had shown me that my work was not as stressful as all that.

Chapter Twelve
Ah, Sweet Mystery of Life
(1972)

I invariably caught the 8:00am train from Taipei station to Neili to direct work at the factory construction site, more so than my city administration office which necessitated my presence less and less as other management functions were taken over by competent locals. My only real setback had faded to insignificance since I had, with US office approval, appointed a replacement local lawyer to replace the one who I had only seen the back of as he leapt from the sixth floor window of his office when I entered the room for our introductory appointment. Thus, the first time we met face to face was when I bowed my head to him dressed in his business suit, he stood in his coffin which was supported at a 60 degree angle giving the impression that he was ready to talk business. I thought this to be tasteless, but it was, I was told, the local custom. Unrequited love from a considerably younger wife and the perceived shame of her infidelity had proved too much for the poor man was the story which emerged from the grapevine.

The morning in question began as usual except that my wife had requested a 7:15 am lift down the steep snaky mountain road to a particular corner to meet friend Audrey at 7:30 since Chen, the driver, was unavailable for work that morning, and she would not therefore be able to have use of the car on that day. "Which corner?" I asked.

"Oh, I will recognise it when I see it," was the reply. I had agreed, providing that she was ready to go promptly to enable me to catch my train. As the car meandered down the many identical tree lined corners, "What time did you agree to meet? I don't have much time to wait, and I can't leave you alone in such a desolate place."

The reply came back from a watchful June, "I think Audrey said 7:30. Stop the car I think this is it. No, carry on." A feeling of foreboding crept over me since all the corners looked identical to me, just upright dense fir trees on either side of the spiralling road. "This is it I think, I recognise that tree, stop the car." I did as I was told, wondering how the hell anyone could recognise one tree out of that lot. No Audrey.

I struggled to remember my manners just as Audrey toddled around the corner and walked to the lowered window of the car and poking her head through, said to June,

"Was this the corner with that tree, and did we say 7:30 or 8.30?" It was the moment I came to realise that I had been reading the wrong books, as without further ado, the two girls strolled away arm in arm. I just had to take a moment to reflect on how the two had met up—neither of them knowing for sure the meeting time or the specific corner they were to meet on. Could two guys have done that? I didn't think so. It bothered me all day.

Chapter Thirteen
A Nonsense of Norms (1957)

Out of the blue and unexpectedly, I received by telephone an invite from a business client to join a select group of engineers to dinner at Parliament House hosted by, as he put it, persons of interest to the food manufacturing industry. Wives of the select group were to be treated to a west end show meanwhile. I booked the company apartment at the Grosvenor Hotel to stay the night arriving in good time to dress for the evening, then on to the foyer of the Hilton Hotel to meet up with the rest of the group. As we walked into the Hilton foyer, I was horrified to see a mass of gentlemen in dinner suits and bow ties, whereas I was in a smart but very light grey Jaeger lounge number with matching accessories. From a distance, I must have resembled a snowball on a heap of coal such was the contrast.

The host approached me and apologised profusely for failing to advise me of the dress code, but there was no way I could attend the dinner dressed like that. With one half hour to dinner time, the situation called for some inventive thinking, "Do you at least have a bow tie with you," asked the host. As we discussed a course of action, a man in greasy overalls walked past them carrying a large toolbox—the lift maintenance engineer as it turned out—and he must have overheard the conversation regarding the bow tie.

He stopped, saying to the two, "Here mate, I think I have a bow tie in my toolbox you can have." Without more ado, he opened his filthy toolbox and started rummaging around pulling out all manner of dirty tools and laying them on the marble floor, I tried to assure the man that although I appreciated his offer, it really wouldn't help the situation, but to no avail.

The floor was littered with tools as he continued to dig deep into his box saying to himself "I know there was one in here because I put it in myself after I used it last." Triumphantly, he held up a greasy brown bow tie and began wiping it on his even greasier overalls. "There you are mate it's yours, I won't need it again anyway." I couldn't refuse it after the effort the guy had made, but wearing it of course was out of the question, the good Samaritan just boxed up his tools and left.

I had an idea. If the host could ferry me back to the Grosvenor, they may just have an emergency dinner suit lying around which I could borrow. Back at the Grosvenor, the concierge grasped the urgency of the situation and hurried me to the wardrobe room where we found all manner of dressage but not a complete suit to fit me, however, he did manage to find a black bow tie and waistcoat, but that was all. Then the concierge asked me what suit I wore to travel to the Grosvenor, and the reply was— dark blue bird's eye. "Better than nothing—wear that with the black waistcoat and bow tie and maybe they won't notice amongst the crowd, worth a try sir.'

Dashing up to the apartment, I did just that, and it didn't look half bad. The concierge grasped his tip as he escorted me to the waiting car for a mad dash back to the Hilton, where the others were in process of boarding the special bus to take them to dinner. 'Just made it.'

The seating arrangements were such that each visitor would be seated with an invited dignitary or a supplier to the food manufacturing industry on either side of him. Polite conversation and introductions were the order of the day, and I struck up an interesting technical discussion with the supplier person to my right. The gentleman on my left, who I had exchanged a few awkward glances with, said nothing, but I had prejudged him as a toff. Suddenly, the toff said in his immaculate high pitched cultured accent, "I say old boy, that is a corking dinner suit you're wearing, is it the latest thing?"

I had to think fast and replied, "Why yes it is—how observant of you to notice." He went on 'must have one, from where did you buy it?' I felt I was digging a hole for myself as the toff again waxed lyrical about my botched up dinner suit.

"Manchester," I said, which was the truth.

"You mean that northerly place?" asked the silver spoon.

"How fascinating. Must make some enquiries."

Chapter Fourteen
The Order of the Flattened Frog (1995)

Without the need to resort to the mass of circumstantial detail as to why the Kenya factory was in such a god awful mess on my arrival, suffice to say that this would be no overstatement. I had expected to find such a mess, the American HQ had told me so when I was hired for a six month last ditch attempt to pull it back from the brink.

Having understood the size of the task, it shouldn't have been a surprise when on my very first morning in the office, I was shaken by a loud explosion as the factory transformer, located within the factory, blew itself to utter destruction, starting a huge fire. There were workers jumping from windows and running in all directions in panic, and for a moment it flashed through my mind that it could be a very short assignment.

The fire brigade arrived after two hours although the factory was but two miles from the city centre, meanwhile the factory fire crew were doing their best with limited equipment and limited water to go with it. It took a further four hours to extinguish the flames by which time damage was quite extensive, and although the critical production areas had escaped with light damage, the power house and workshops were gutted, prohibiting production. One month passed before power was reconnected allowing time for me to get a firm grip of the problems and formulate a plan of action.

Technical matters aside, although these were many, a major part of the whole problem was the factory staffing. For instance, I discovered that ninety percent of the workers came from one small district of Nairobi, also that it was a fully unionised crew who took their orders directly from the Union headquarters situated in downtown Nairobi, not the factory management. The Union CEO was receiving a ten percent cash kickback directly from all workers within the factory in addition to Union dues to enable them to keep their jobs. This was red flag to a bull as far as I was concerned but the scam was very well entrenched and extremely difficult to counter. The Kenyan business management team knew of the situation but were powerless to act since high level governmental politics were involved, and if they valued their jobs, they had better keep quiet. Immediately, following the fire, I had noticed that the Union CEO had held meetings in the factory yard with the workers who were still being paid the basic wage even though production was temporarily closed down. Matters came to a head when one week following the fire, the Union chief barged into my office unannounced and was immediately shown the door and told to wait outside until he was summoned. On re-entering the office, war was officially declared between myself and the Union.

My plan was basically simple. First, solve the many technical shortcomings within the operation, meanwhile gathering data and evidence of Union wrongdoings to build a foundation for change which was critical to the survival of the factory.

As operation shortcomings were progressively overcome, the more intelligent engineers and operators within the factory, and there were a few, began to realise the potential of the factory, and I was making essential allies to a point where I was able to get rid of the dross despite Union objections. I was attending the industrial courts every week to fight wrongful dismissal charges but was gradually winning the battle to improve the quality of staff. I now had allies who would testify against the Unions counterclaims. A key move was made to improve the female toilet and shower facilities which were previously not fit for a pig to live in. I was in fact told that I was the first male ever to enter the ladies' facilities which was taboo to the local males, even for cleaning or repairs. Females within the factory were previously treated very poorly, but improvements to their pay rates and facilities produced a transformation in their performance. The Union chief could not get his head around the growing anger towards him by his previously obedient sheep, and I was receiving ominous threats by telephone. One example of Union desperation was to have one of his few remaining loyal followers scatter raw meat around the entrance to the workplace which the locals would not cross because of taboo. They would not touch the meat, and I had to clear this myself following which normal working resumed.

The situation progressed to a point which produced the almost unbelievable request from a delegation of workers that they wanted rid of the union in favour of a factory committee, elected by them. Already the Union CEO had stopped visiting the factory, and although I was delighted with the turnaround, I knew that there would be high hurdles to climb to achieve my ambitious goal.

The dirty tricks were not long in materialising. First, there appeared in the national newspaper an article calling for my deportation on the grounds that I was trying to crush the people's representative unions, there to fight against the exploitation of workers by management. There were acts of sabotage in the factory by the one or two still loyal (due to monetary favours) to the union. However, they were summarily dismissed on being reported causing further wrongful dismissal cases, but the writing was now on the wall, and the crunch came when there was a formal request from the elected committee to withdraw entirely from their union. Absolutely unheard of.

The works committee and I were summoned to appear before—not the industrial court, but the Department of Industrial Affairs, who were responsible for the wellbeing of all workers in Kenya—a quasi-governmental organisation overseeing all industrial affairs in the country, including keeping a watchful but impartial eye on union activities. A highly important organisation on the industrial scene. There were some twenty or so persons present including lawyers from both sides, and each representative was able to state their case to the chairman, including myself, when I congratulated the workers for their contribution to the vast improvement in factory performance and stressed that the request to leave the union had come from themselves. A stillness descended on the assembly awaiting the chairman's reply.

Looking directly at me, he said, "You know sir that this matter can only be resolved in the high industrial court, and my organisation would be pleased to continue to represent your company and the wishes of your employees. You should also understand that the unions in this country are very powerful and aggressive and are well connected politically. They can be likened to a big mad dog if challenged in this way, and how can you beat such a dog."

I was inwardly seething at the obvious capitulation of the chairman and replied, 'Well in that case sir, we shall just need to find a bigger dog." That concluded the meeting.

The issue resolved itself when, having sought good advice, I was directed to a prominent local lawyer who won the case in the industrial court before an obviously biased panel of judges plus the loud ranting of the union CEO. The latter, in desperation at the way the case was going, announced that his office had never received written cancellation notices from each individual member, despite such notices having been sent separately by post, by DHL courier, and by hand to the union office showing his secretary's signature of receipt. That was his final undoing which even the biased judge could not condescend. My original theory that the union would be unable to win the case if both I and the union CEO were riding the same horse i.e. the welfare of the employees and the betterment of their pay and working conditions was proved correct, since the union was only effective when the opposite was true.

Back in my office, the first morning following the verdict, I slid into my desk chair only to catch my knee on some obstruction on the underside of the desk. Reaching beneath, I could feel a nail which had been hammered in, holding an object which I withdrew having managed to loosen the nail.

It was a large well flattened dried frog spread-eagled like road kill, but very recognisable for what it was. Summoning my secretary, she told me that it was the highest honour which could be paid to anyone to receive a flattened frog, obviously put there by the new works committee in thanks.

Needless to say, my wife refused to add the trophy to her display cabinet, but we did stay in Kenya for eight years.

Chapter Fifteen
A Case for Automation (1958)

The year was 1958, and the smokeless zones act was by then well established and making a positive contribution to the quality of the air that we breathe. The Ringelmann chart then devised to estimate the density of smoke emitted from industrial chimneys was widely used in the absence of anything better, although it was a method primarily subject to interpretation. All this theory was lost on the ladies of Ellesmere Road whose houses backed onto the colliery rail road which ferried coal from the mine to the storage depot a dozen or more times per day, belching filthy black smoke and cinders over their washing lines as the steam locomotives passed.

They had been protesting via petitions and numerous delegations to the local authorities and the National Coal Board itself to do something to eradicate the threat to their shirts and smalls. The case had now reached the tribunal stage, and a hefty fine was virtually certain to be levied on the NCB.

I, as a management trainee with the NCB, was otherwise occupied and totally unaware of the case and ignorant of the facts, that is until I was summoned to the office of the chief engineer who greeted me not with the usual "How are you getting on with your training," but with "Can you drive a locomotive" which rather took me aback. I was 24 years old at the time, and the nearest I had been to a steam loco was when at age 18 as an apprentice in the central workshops I had been sent to the loco repair shed to brew ten cans (tin flasks) of tea utilising the sand drying stove to boil a huge pan of water to do the necessary, which ended in disaster. Without thinking, I had removed the lids from the flasks and put them in line on to the locomotive stationery behind me. After I had filled all the cans from the heavy boiling pan, I turned around to collect the lids, but the loco had silently gone taking the lids with it.

It is difficult today to convey just how sacrosanct the brew can was to their owners. I was petrified of having to return the steaming cans without their lids but had no option but to do so. I received a deserved thrashing and was dispatched down the railway track to retrieve the lids which I eventually managed to do. It took a while for me to live that one down.

Before I could reply to the question from the chief, came the instruction, "Report to the loco sheds on Monday morning and teach the drivers there how to drive without producing filthy smoke, and submit a weekly report of your progress. That is all for now." I left the office straining my mind to recollect my theoretical thermo dynamics which was all I had to go by.

As instructed, I reported sharp at 6am at the loco sheds and commenced to don my work overalls amongst the other drivers who cast enquiring looks in my direction, but nothing was said until the foreman driver and shop steward of the National Affiliated Locomotive Drivers Union arrived. "Who are you?" he asked.

"Oh I am the representative of the Area Chief Engineer sent to advise you on how to drive your locos efficiently." The foreman's face turned a pale shade of purple, but he cooled down a little when he was shown the authority document.

"What experience have you got of loco driving young fellow," he asked.

"None at all" came the truthful reply, at which stage the foreman went almost apoplectic, "but I do know the theory," I flashed back, having refreshed my thermo dynamics over the weekend.

"In that case you can teach me first—you'll ride with me. Let's go."

On the footplate with the foreman and his driver, I instructed them to do what they always did to enable me to assess their method. The rail track to the depot was inclined at a 10% rise, and it was therefore imperative that sufficient steam pressure was maintained during the five mile trip. If not, then there was the distinct chance that the weight of the coal filled wagons would accede to gravity and overcome the loco, dragging it back down the slope with disastrous consequences. I observed the various gauges in the cab, noticing the absence of a draught gauge, which in my opinion, was essential to economic handling of combustion control. The foreman driver and his stoker piled on the coal right from the start and continued to do so throughout the trip, bodies soaked with perspiration at the effort. They eventually reached the top of the incline having dumped nothing short of half a ton of coal dust on the ladies washing lines. Having demonstrated to me how laborious their job was and why they deserved their wages and conditions, they hooked up empty wagons and coasted back down to bottom of the incline to pick up another load.

This time, I requested that they should work to my instructions. This they did and completed the trip using half of the coal from previous time and emitting virtually no chimney coal dust to aggravate the ladies. In fact, some of the ladies were attending to their washing lines en route and cheered and clapped to the loco as it sailed past. "Nothing magic about it," I told the crew. "Just good combustion practice."

I explained my method to the two men who had, as a result, needed to work half as hard, and I certainly got their attention on that score alone. To complete my assignment, I had a draught gauge fitted to the cabs of all the locos and instructed the drivers how to use it in conjunction with the Geisel ejector to provide economic and efficient combustion conditions.

On my last trip with the drivers having earned my stripes in their eyes, I told the shop steward that I thought I could automate my system, and the steward nearly fainted when I further told him that automation would save one man per loco. The foreman watched my finger intently as I traced out the pipe work route within the cab to operate the automation.

"How does it work," he asked?

I replied, "Quite simple really! The small copper pipe provides a draught gauge reading to the back of the cab behind the stoker's head where it is connected to a two pound hammer, and if the stoker piles too much coal on the fire, the hammer smacks him on the back of his head." I was inaugurated into the National Affiliated Locomotive Drivers Union as an honorary member.

Chapter Sixteen
Make Way! Make Way! (1996)

I had been hosting the American corporate hierarchy of a multinational company, being at that time in charge of their Kenya operation. They had done all the usual safari trips, held all honorary banquets and the like and were now departing to board the company jet back to Chicago. They were due to take off at 8am on the Monday morning, and I had arranged to see them away, which meant my having to be at the airport before 7:30am at the latest. Daniel, my driver, was at my home early, and we left at 6:45am which would mean arrival at the airport at 7:15am.

My company car was the then latest Land Rover Discovery in white, and driver Daniel was chauffer dressed complete with peak cap. As we drove towards the airport, we ran into heavy traffic due to a road accident causing severe congestion. The car did not move an inch during the next 30 minutes, the road ahead was well and truly jammed with trucks, cars and Matatu buses, no way through, and no way out, since it was similarly jammed behind us. I was reading my morning *Nation* newspaper in the rear and called out to Daniel to please do something to get us out of the total confusion and do his best to make the airport which was still some seven miles distant. Daniel's options were limited to say the least, but to him, an instruction was an instruction, and without more ado, he pulled the vehicle off the road and into the pedestrian area amongst stalls of vegetables and whatnot, scattering stallholders and customers, with people and produce going in all directions. Suddenly, we were stopped by the raised arms of two policemen, one of whom approached the car, whereupon Daniel lowered his window. In the rear, hidden behind my newspaper, I heard the policeman shouting at Daniel in good English. "Why are you putting this man (meaning me) in such danger? Don't you know that this man is a good friend to Kenya and you are trying to kill him, you should be ashamed of yourself." I could see that Daniel was shaking like a leaf in fear of the police. Then addressing me, who did not show my face around my newspaper, the policeman said, "Please accept my sincere apologies sir, where are you going to?'

I murmured, "The airport, urgently.' It then dawned on me that the policeman had mistaken my car for the British ambassador's car which was identical, made more so by the two union flag stickers on the sides of my vehicle. No more ado the two policemen started to clear a path through the pedestrian area in front of Daniel. For more than a mile they shoved aside stalls, people and anything else in the way to allow the car through the jam until it emerged into the clear road in front. I acknowledged the divine intervention of the saluting police officers by waving one hand through my side window in a royal manner but not showing my face from behind the newspaper.

When we were in the clear, I lowered my newspaper to see Daniel's back heaving and shaking—not in fear this time but in uncontrollable laughter.

We arrived at the airport just in time for me to be spared the embarrassment of not being able to bid my eminent visitors farewell.

Chapter Seventeen
Economic Policing Made Easy (1971)

I had been collected from O Hare airport and was being driven to my hotel by Frank and Cathy, American friends and work colleagues. The car radio played gentle music, and the surround sound was wafting it around my ears in the back seat. Suddenly, the music was interrupted by a harsh voice announcing the shooting dead of two people in down town Chicago. Frank called out, bewailing the ever escalating crime rate in the city which the police seemed unable to control despite the high number of officers on the streets. I asked why the US didn't take a leaf out of the Taipei policeman's book since their city crime rate was very low—the streets being very safe to walk around even at night. Frank asked me to elaborate on my statement which I did, saying that in Taiwan, the only punishment for any crime was to be shot by firing squad without leave to appeal, and this had had a tremendous deterrent effect on anyone contemplating committing an offence. Frank retorted that that could never pass muster in the States because too many innocent people would be wrongly imprisoned or executed.

I said that you had to do the maths to justify the system, but the results would show that many lives would be saved.

I went on to say that if you were to compare the number of people killed in Chicago through crime, to the number of people wrongly executed, the system would speak for itself.

Frank was listening intently to all this while keeping his eyes on the road. "No, no we couldn't do that," he said, "but it does make a certain amount of sense. Just how many people are wrongly executed in Taiwan every year then Don—would you have a number on that?"

"Statistics show that only 30% of people arrested were wrongly shot, and that seems a pretty acceptable average. I replied, "Don't you think it's worth thinking about Frank?"

"It sounds common sense alright," said Frank, "but have you seen any proof that it's only 30%? It may just be a political number."

Just as Frank said that, the news announcer again broke into the music to say that Reuters reported that Taiwan had just executed three men for murder, one of whom had posthumously been found to be innocent.

"There you are Frank, what more proof do you need?" However, I could not keep the nonsense up any longer, and my laughter was joined by the two in the front seat, and we laughed and laughed the rest of the way to the hotel. The coincidence of the moment was superb.

Chapter Eighteen
With Jesus as My Guide (1998)

I had taken my wife to Ngulia safari lodge in West Tsavo National Park for a few days R&R, and as usual the local wildlife had not disappointed. Our intention was to travel on to Amboseli and Kilimanjaro to complete the week, a drive I had not previously done, but which the sketchy map did show to be possible. Speaking with the local Ngulia park guides, I was strongly advised to hire a travel guide for security and directional advice. Around noon, we set off on our journey and before long arrived at the barrier situated at the guard outpost, where I entered and requested to hire a guard/guide. It occurred to me that such a request was something unusual to the three uniformed men, since they began to talk among themselves in Swahili and looked a little puzzled at the request. This was confirmed when none of the three could agree as to what to charge for the service. Eventually, a fee was agreed, and my wife was requested to take the rear car seat allowing the selected guard to ride shotgun next to me in front. Not a shotgun, in fact, but a Kalashnikov, the sight of which startled my wife who began to express doubts about the wisdom of the trip.

The soldier—I had by this time recognised that he was no park warden—understood English for when he was asked his name, he replied 'Jesus' which put my mind at rest a little since I could not imagine a bandit sporting that name.

The road soon deteriorated to a bumpy track, but the four wheel vehicle had no difficulty in making good progress through the desolate landscape. After some time through no man's land, small shanty villages started to appear, and the guard asked if we could take a diversion to deliver the military post which was in his rucksack. I now understood what all the jabber was about in the guard post before leaving. It concerned the opportunity to deliver the soldiers' post to their various remote locations situated on the hills they were driving through. Jesus held his gun up to the side window to deter any villagers from encroaching on the car as they detoured through the now increasingly inhabited areas, dropping off post as they went to soldiers at the various barrier gates.

Finally, having added a good two hours to our journey, we arrived at a sizable army camp where the barrier guards were less than friendly to Jesus who they didn't seem to recognise as one of them, and guns were cocked at the car startling the occupants. I asked Jesus to step out of the car and show the guard the post in his rucksack which he did, and suddenly, it was Christmas time. The soldiers who I surmised must not have received any post for some considerable time went wild with joy delving into the postbag being joined by others running from the barracks. Jesus now became the hero, and much back slapping was going on when I reminded Jesus that he was on hire, and they had a journey to complete, preferably before the impending dusk. The barracks soldiers however had other ideas and persuaded Jesus to join the revelry and sod the tour guide hire. Somewhat outnumbered, I gave up trying to get Jesus to obey my commandments and settled for onward directions to Amboseli which seemed pretty straightforward from where we were on the summit of the hills approaching Kilimanjaro, which could be seen in the distance. So, off we set to the cheers of the soldiers.

I was very familiar with the western approaches to Amboseli but had no knowledge whatsoever of the eastern approach I was now taking, and darkness was overtaking us. I also knew that the entrance gates to the safari park were closed to visitors at 5pm. Travelling as fast as I dared, I reached visual sighting of the East gate with five minutes to spare, headlights blazing. As I neared the gate, I could see the gate staff locking up the gates from the outside and drifting off to home. Honking my horn and flashing my lights, I reached the gate and jumped out of the car in time to call back the gatekeeper, who was not very happy to return to his kiosk but did so following entreaties. He unlocked the gates, took the entrance fee and tip and booked us into the park, then, as was routine, telephoned the lodge to expect us to arrive. Darkness falls quickly at these latitudes, and keeping to the designated tracks through the park, we had made two or three miles before complete darkness created a surrounding eerie feeling to the park. No sounds save the tyres on the dirt track and strange shapes outlined in the headlights. I had never before driven in total darkness in any safari park, and not being familiar with Amboseli East terrain added to my concern. I was looking for some guidance from the hit and miss signposting but it was scant, and no mention of the Serena Lodge had I seen so far.

Thirty minutes later, I was no nearer to being comfortable as to the direction I was travelling, and my wife was getting more and more anxious. No mobile phones in those days, but I surmised that the lodge would inform the park rangers if we failed to arrive.

Gradually, the foliage disappeared from the car headlights, and we were off road on barely visible track across the seemingly endless dessert like wastes of the massive dry lake bed. The track had disappeared, and I slowed to a crawl since I was well aware of the dangers on these flatbeds and tried to pick up any track I could find without success. Then I spotted a light in the far distance. Only a glimmer, but it was definitely a light probably from a lodge—not necessarily the lodge I was looking for, but it meant safety for the night, and I steered the car in that direction travelling at no more than ten miles per hour on full beam headlights. Then we hit a patch of dense mist which could only mean that water was close by, and I had to dispense with the full beam which was being thrown back into the car by the mist. In fact, I could hardly see the ground in front of me. A little further on and I couldn't see out of the car at all which was scary, and my wife was hidden under a blanket in the rear seat. Suddenly, I felt the slow moving car rock a little from side to side which I put down to uneven ground but continued to progress onwards now at five miles per hour, hoping to get through the mist patch to enable me to see the distant light once more, but it seemed endless going at the speed I was going. The car again rocked from side to side, but this time, I was sure that I was being pushed by something. I was! I was in the centre of a large herd of elephants travelling in the same direction.

The mist finally began to thin out which meant to me that we must be moving away from water, and I was able to switch on my full headlights again. The sight which met my eyes started my adrenaline flowing. The car was right in the middle of twenty or so elephants ranging from huge to babies, on the move in their slow plodding fashion at my five miles an hour. With the beasts on either side and front and back, I had no room for manoeuvre, and I was being ultra-careful not to alarm them particularly the young, one of which was virtually leaning on the car as it lumbered along. They did not seem to mind the car lights which were floodlighting the scene now that they were clear of the mist, and I was hoping that they were going towards Serena lodge. For what seemed like an age, the unlikely retinue plodded on until I slowed the car down to a crawl steering slightly to my left, away from the close up elephant on my right, hoping that the herd would gradually overtake me, leaving me in the clear. It took a while but eventually that is what happened, and my headlights were able to show the full size of the herd which was heart stopping.

The light that I had spotted over to my left side was now clearly visible, together with the shadowy outline of the lodge— it was the Serena lodge, and it was but a ten minute drive before we arrived at the front entrance. I had no idea how I managed to get the car into the middle of the herd without colliding with at least one elephant being the size they were. Granted I was driving very slowly and warily, but even so it could have ended in disaster when I think of the consequences of my colliding with the strolling herd.

Chapter Nineteen
The 200mph Wind (1972)

The USA 327th Air Division in Taipei had sent out over the radio an approaching cyclone warning over the past two days. Except for the American presence on the island, there would have been no English language warning to alert the ex pats of the impending super storm. The word around the cocktails circuit was that wind speeds could reach 200 miles per hour, although several know all said that the only thing super about the storm was the exaggerated wind speed. The storm was expected to hit over the weekend, so at least families should be together, and all events and cocktail parties were cancelled over the two days, since weather forecasting in those days was sketchy to say the least.

The rain from a blackened sky began on the Saturday morning, heavy and persistent. That was not unusual for Taipei at that time of year, the wind was blowing but nothing out of the ordinary, by noon, it had got no worse, and people were saying "Is that all there is" the know-alls were right—typical American exaggeration, but the Chinese house staff were fidgety.

I and my wife and two children lived high on Yang Ming Shan, the mountain overlooking the city, in theological college grounds where all the single story houses were constructed of black granite stone blocks with concrete slab roofs. The only vulnerable structures were the bamboo built car ports, (mine was on my concrete roof,) and conservatories. By 1pm, the wind was picking up, and if I thought that the sky was black that morning, it turned to ink after noon. Never had we seen skies like that before, the rain was torrential and increasingly horizontal then total darkness descended. The noise of the wind was now deafening, and myself and family went into another rear bedroom behind closed wooden shuttered windows, but it was impossible to speak to each other due to the screeching wind. The children clung to me and my wife was terrified—particularly, when we heard the conservatory shatter and the sounds of breaking glass and furniture toppling coming from the living area. It lasted for two hours before it suddenly stopped as though it had been switched off, and daylight returned. I went out through the west facing front door to a beautiful sunny clear blue sky, still, not a breath of wind, also not a sound from the usually noisy, bountiful insect and frog population in the semi tropical foliage. I knew it was the eye of the storm passing directly over us, I also knew that the furious wind would return from the reverse direction once the eye had passed. I ran around the house perimeter to assess the damage, noting that the car port had gone, the conservatory was badly damaged, my car had been pushed into the hedgerow, and windows were broken. Trees and branches were everywhere, covering my roof and driveway, including the many steps up to roof level which was our only way out. The silence lasted for twenty minutes or so, and I was still outside trying to sort things out a bit when I felt the wind pick up a little, and inky skies could be seen moving quickly from the west. The house living area had some water on the terrazzo laid floors blown in through the damaged windows, but I had expected worse. The worst was to come however as darkness once again descended, and I moved the family into the rear bedroom to sit out the remainder of the tempest. Screaming like a banshee, the noise of the wind hurt our ears which we had to cover with our hands.

In the rear garden, there was a substantial tree which I could just about encircle with my arms, situated some three yards from the rear wall of the bedroom we were in. The wind reached a crescendo and started to bend the tree in gusts, and it was thumping the concrete slab roof with terrific bangs. Added to that, the wind was now blowing the rain right through the granite wall blocks of the bedroom like a waterfall which was rapidly flooding the room. I had no option but to move the family to the front living area where there was less water. The cyclone petered out a couple of hours later, when it gradually subsided to torrential rain and the wind to a stiff breeze. Eventually, something resembling daylight returned.

Having spent a soggy night with little sleep, I rescued my car and cleared the pile of tree branches and foliage covering everything around to enable me to get out of the compound and drive down the mountain road into the city to hopefully buy some essentials. The whole city was flooded—roofs were gone, and the whole area was littered with shop signs and advertising hoarding. The US base radio station was transmitting giving advice and offering medical assistance information, stating that they had clocked the wind velocity in excess of 200mph. The continuous torrential rain had created another more sinister menace—that of deadly snakes washed out of the undergrowth and on to pedestrian areas. Taiwan snakes varied in length from short to over two metres and were referred to by the locals as one minuters up to one dayers, which was the time you had before death if bitten. The majority of the numerous snakes didn't bother you if you didn't bother them, but there were exceptions. I killed one snake a week on average, and there was the occasion when my eight year old daughter screamed from the rear garden causing me to run to see a black mamba about four feet long chasing her around the lawn. Picking up rock, I chased the snake, and though I missed with my first throw, it caused the reptile to veer away from the pursuit of the little girl. Now I was chasing the snake, but it beat me to the undergrowth and disappeared. The speed of the snake was surprisingly quick. Vigilance was always the watchword, and the whole family were aware of that. My wife was terrified of them which didn't help matters, but like the rest of the community, she gradually got used to their presence. The reason why there was such a proliferation and variety of deadly snakes at that time was due, it was said, to the presence on the island of the Japanese during the Second World War where they imported the most deadly of snakes from the war zones surrounding Burma to manufacture antidotes to protect their troops. Following their ousting from Taiwan, they simply turned the reptiles loose to infest the island. Despite the threat, during my three years on the island, the ex pat community only lost one person to the snakes. One New Zealand girl attending a late night barbeque wearing fashionable but open toed sandals, which all the ladies knew, was not the thing to do. We heard that she stepped on a five minuter.

Following the super cyclone, the skies remained dark grey with continuous heavy drizzling rain for six weeks with not a break in the cloud. The damage to property and the clearing up process was tackled efficiently and quickly by the local authorities in typical hard working Taiwanese fashion—very impressive. More importantly, all the washed out snakes had returned to their habitat. Experiencing a 200mph wind etches an indelible memory on the mind and certainly reemphasises the potential power of the air that we breathe.

Chapter Twenty
The Land of Smiles (1978)

No not Thailand but Ireland. I had never been there before on business or pleasure but had now received instructions from head office to travel there to conduct the technical evaluation of a prospective acquisition for the parent US Company.

I was met at Dublin airport by the HR manager of the company which was located some twenty miles west of the city, but initial discussions would be held at the Gresham hotel where I would be staying. The post meeting evening dinner was memorable for the number and variety of Irish coffees were consumed by the assembled guests. I had never had Irish coffee before and was unaware of the alcoholic content which my hosts did not disclose to me until late in the evening. Finally, getting bleary eyed to my room way after midnight, I fell into a deep sleep, only to be rudely awakened in the early hours by a tremendous explosion which shook the room and everything in it. I jumped out of bed and felt my way to the door whereupon I was met with the sight of guests running up and down the corridor in their night attire. My initial hazy thinking was that the hotel boiler was the cause of the explosion, for there was no staff to be seen ushering people out of their rooms, and being as tired as I was, I just went back to my bed and fell asleep.

The following morning at breakfast, nothing seemed untoward, and I collected my briefcase and made my way to the taxi rank. I approached a driver who was polishing the top of his cab furiously. "Good morning, can you take me to the Clarnico confectionery factory please?" The driver looked at me smiling broadly while continuing to polish with gusto. "We blewed a statue up last night we did. He's gone he is.

Nelson's gone." It was then that I noticed a pile of rubble where the statue of Nelson had stood in front of the hotel, which explained the explosion. The driver was full of glee, not taking the slightest notice of my request. "The sun's never shone on the top of my taxi before in all these years I've parked here, and now it has," as he continued to rub his roof.

"Glory be! Glory be!" I felt I couldn't share in the taxi driver's euphoria, and besides, my head was still thumping a little from my introduction to the local coffee, so I walked on to the next taxi where the driver was sitting in the car.

"Do you know the Clarnico Factory, can you take me there please?" The man turned his head towards me and started to sing a nationalist song. I wondered if I was ever going to get into work that morning, so I opened the taxi door and climbed in. The taxi moved away with the driver still singing loudly, then when we had gone about a mile the taxi driver turned to me and said, "Where do you want to go to young sir?"

The managing director of the factory was a very pleasant intelligent chap who gave his full assistance during the whole of that day, and I felt that I had achieved what I was sent to do. At 5pm, the MD offered me a lift back into Dublin city to my hotel, which I gratefully accepted since the factory was well out into rural countryside. At the last moment, before they left the factory, the MD said that his wife had telephoned him causing him to have to drive in the opposite direction, which nullified my lift into Dublin. However, he would be able to take me to the taxi rank close by the factory which was fine by me. Taxi rank! What taxi rank? It turned out to be a small lay by aside the Dublin road. No taxis in site, no vehicles on the road, no people in sight, no buildings either. Saying that there would be a taxi along soon, the MD said his farewells and drove off. Dusk turned to darkness one hour later, and I was still waiting for a taxi or indeed any vehicle to turn up and was feeling a bit miserable under my black umbrella in the cold drizzle. Then out of the misty darkness loomed a double deck bus, and not caring where it was going, I flagged it down.

The bus conductor leaned out from the ancient looking bus deck, and I asked him if he was bound for Dublin. In a heavily accented reply which I did not comprehend, he beckoned me on to the bus, which remained stationery while the conductor had a chat with me about where I came from and what I was doing in such a remote area after dark. All the passengers inside the lower deck were craning their necks to listen in on the conversation. Then I asked the conductor if the bus was going anywhere near the Gresham Hotel whereupon the man threw his hands in the air saying that he had never before had anyone from the Gresham on his bus. Finally, he punched the long brass rod which rang the bell in the driver's cab as I climbed the stairway to the upper deck. The bus rattled along for a few miles, before the conductor came up the stairs to collect the fares. When he reached my seat and was offered the fare, he said in a loud voice, "No sir no sir, nobody from the Gresham pays on my bus, it's my honour." I was now stared at by all on the upper deck who were probably discussing why they had to pay and muttering in dissent.

The lights of the outskirts of the city were now in view, and the bus made a couple of stops before a loud cry came from the lower deck. "Would the young gentleman from the Gresham please come down?" I arrived on the lower platform to find the conductor furiously punching on the bell rod, and the bell could be clearly heard ringing continuously. "He's got a divil of a mood on him today sir—we blewed a statue up last night you know sir, and I can't stop him."

Hanging out from the platform, the conductor said, "Jump off sir when I tell you—he's not going to stop." The bus was travelling slowly enough, and both myself and the conductor were hanging out to look ahead, when the instruction came, "Now sir, God be with you sir," as I jumped clutching my briefcase. Following a mazy walk through the back streets of Dublin, I finally found my hotel.

Ten years had passed before I had the need to revisit the emerald isle on business, but I was, or at least I thought I would be better prepared to meet the cultural norms. This time I was there to discuss future company strategy in Ireland with the local directorate, also to attend a conference on business opportunities in the country. From my catholic upbringing, I had been schooled in Irish traditions and music by my northern family and their Celtic friends and felt confident that I knew enough about the culture to have my advice listened to as being a useful contribution to the cause. In the event, my sense of humour would again prove to be my most valuable asset, more so than my technical expertise.

Having boarded the Holyhead overnight ferry, I went to my cabin, stored my baggage and made my way to the bar for a nightcap. Later, having retired for the night, I managed to drift into some form of sleep, I was jolted bolt upright in my bunk when the engine started, which caused the oscillating 'big end' to be thumped repeatedly into the underside of the cabin floor, shaking the room to bits and making unbearable noise. It being impossible to sleep, I dressed and returned to the bar, where I saw passengers sleeping on the floor, on chairs, in fact all over the place, all except one, a Scotsman drinking at the bar. There was no one tending the bar, but the drinker had his own bottle and was well away, singing to himself, and beckoning me to join him. The man roared with laughter when I explained why I had left the cabin. Apparently, no one ever booked the cabin on that small ferry since there was only one, situated over the engine room, which explained the passengers sleeping in the bar.

"Your second trip to Ireland is it then laddie," the man said in his broad accent made more unintelligible by his inebriated state, "they are all robbers over there, aye, all robbers the lot of them."

He went on to illustrate his point by telling me of his recent trip to Sligo on business. Having purchased a first class train ticket from Dublin to Sligo, he arrived at his platform to find that there was no first class carriage in the train. Challenging the station master, he was told the reason, being that there was 'no call for them sir, no call for them at all.' Showing his first class ticket to the official, he was referred back to the ticket office. The ticket seller said, "But didn't you ask for a first class ticket, and didn't I give you what you asked for sir?"

The frustrated Scotsman fired back, "Did you not know that the first class service had been removed?" The teller replied, "Oh yes sir, because there is no call for them sir."

I was met by a local official of the company who was to drive me to his factory destination to attend the 10am board meeting, a ninety minute drive away from Dublin I was told. General business chat ensued between us, and I was suitably impressed by John's pleasant and professional manner, also his knowledge of the business. Half an hour into the journey, John suddenly changed the subject. "I've bought myself a racehorse sir so I have. Do you like horses' sir?" I am most definitely not a horsy person, although I had always been civil in their company, I thought it would diplomatic not to mention the fact that I knew nothing whatsoever about horses and their keep, so in reply said, "I like other peoples' horses alright John."

John beamed at this and pulled the sucker question. "Will I show you my horse, he's a fine looking animal, and with a small diversion we have time to check on him, will I do that sir?" A feeling of apprehension crept over me as I nodded agreement, remembering that I was in the land of the unvarnished understatement, wondering what I had let myself in for. The feeling was emphasised when we ran into a black sky thunderstorm with torrential rain, and John had just turned off the main road on to a farm track. Slowly, the car made its way down the track until it stopped at a five barred gate at the side of a field, hedged around its perimeter with hawthorn. The rain was heavier than ever, and John put his suit coat over his head and asking me to do likewise got out of the car and went to the gate. I was in business attire and so was reticent to do so, but I did have a mackintosh in the rear seat and used that as a cape to cover my head, then followed John to the gate. It certainly was a fine looking racehorse, but it was standing in the middle of a freshly ploughed field in the pouring rain, looking completely bewildered. John shouted out loud, "Jesus and Mary he's ploughed the f***in' field." Obviously, it must have been grassed when John last saw it.

"I must catch him, I have to catch him," shouted a very distressed John, and without further ado, he jumped over the gate into a sea of mud and ran towards the horse, which bolted and proceeded to gallop around the field throwing up a wake of wet soil, with John in pursuit. I watched the uneven contest for five minutes or so, but the rain and bitterly cold wind was getting to me, and I went back to the car and huddled down trying to dry out, cursing the moment I agreed to see the horse.

A full hour passed without John's return, and though I went back to the gate, there was no sign of John or the horse. Eventually, a bedraggled and mud covered John returned to the car and slid into the driver seat. "Don't worry sir, I caught him and took him back to the farm." Don't worry! That was the understatement of the day.

"What about the board meeting John, it will be over before we get there." By now, I should have anticipated the reply, "Don't worry sir, the others will wait for us, fine fellows the lot o' them."

I resigned myself to the situation, as the car resumed its journey reaching the factory one hour later, two hours late for the meeting. I was warmly received by the three other board members without any mention of what caused the delay, or indeed why John's suit and shoes were covered in mud. Pleasantries abounded—they certainly made me most welcome. As they took their seats at the board table, this was reinforced when a pint bottle of Guinness was plonked before everyone at the table by a smiling young lady who then followed up with platters of bites. I was a little taken aback and hoped that I was not expected to drink a pint of Guinness at 12noon. I politely refused to do so, but the rest of the members had no such reservations and were quickly into their second bottle. This seemed to have no adverse effect on the participants, and the business was successfully concluded in the next hour. Lunch at the crowded local pub was an experience. There was a full Irish band, lots of singing and copious drinking, and I was the only one capable of walking a straight line by 3pm, when everyone emerged into the car park. This was 1977, and the drink driving law was not rigidly enforced, at least no one seemed to pay attention to the fact. The two cars carrying me and my hosts back to the factory were haring towards Dublin when the leading car ground to a halt, and our car pulled up behind. Dr Russell walked back to our car and spoke to the driver through the side window. "Bejabers I'm driving the wrong way, I should be driving west. See you all in the morning. Nice meeting you, have a safe journey home,"

While dining at my small town hotel in the evening, I asked the receptionist where I could hire a car from since I would need to drive myself to the conference centre in two days' time. "Oh, you'll be wanting the butchers," she said.

"The butchers?" I asked quizzically.

"Why the butchers?" The girl looked at me as though it was me who had asked the daft question.

"Because don't you know he has the only car for rental in town." I hesitated, not able to follow the logic, but nevertheless asked for directions to the butchers, which proved to be two doors down from the hotel. The following morning, I strolled slowly to the butchers and looking through the window could see the owner thrashing a carcass of meat on his block and a couple of customers waiting. Not wanting to make a fool of myself in front the customers in case it was a setup, I strolled away then returned and entered the shop.

"You've come to the right place for the best car in town sir, she's a fine runner," said the butcher as he carried on chopping his meat.

"We'll have it ready for you at nine tomorrow morning sir, on the dot sir."

I arrived outside the butchers shop promptly at 9am to find a young man polishing a tatty twenty-year-old Mini. Entering the shop, I was greeted by the butcher. "Top of the morning to you sir, your car is ready for you." My expression told the butcher of my displeasure but was breezily told, "Don't worry sir", where had I heard that before? "It's a fine runner, it won't let you down." Not having a choice, I showed my UK driving licence and asked if I could pay something extra to cover insurance.

"Oh, we don't worry about things like that, sir. No, sir. You just take the car and bring it back when you're finished with it." In a mild state of shock, I opened my wallet and asked how much for the day.

"You can give me a couple of quid when you bring the car back; that will be fine, sir." I realised at that moment that I was trying too hard and stopped trying to think rationally.

A 'when in Rome' feeling crept over me, and I drove away having eventually managing to find first gear.

The conference centre was a splendid looking place, and as I drove along the frontage, the cars parked there were Jaguars, Mercedes, Range Rovers and the like. There was no one around, so I drove the Mini banger around the corner of the building out of sight. Having struck up conversations with other attendees as they strolled out of the conference, I waited till everyone had driven away in their limousines before sneaking around the corner to my battered bus.

The butcher's shop was still trading when I arrived back, and I parked in front then entered to return the keys. "Everything fine for you, sir?" to which I assented and gave the butcher a fiver. I then pocketed the three pounds change and left.

Chapter Twenty-One
The New Village Chief (1992)

If I had harboured any ambitions as a young man, then certainly furthest from my thoughts would have been that I would become the Chief of a Fijian village in the South Pacific Ocean.

I was on vacation there with my wife and two young grandsons and had booked a safari to visit an untouched Fijian village far from civilisation. Arriving at the departure point, we met up with the other twenty or so men, women and children who had booked the same trip. Mostly American and Australian, they made themselves known when they raised their hands in response to a request from the Fijian guide.

"Any English?" shouted the guide, to which I raised a lone hand and was duly appointed the chief of the invading mob. I didn't know at that time what I had let myself in for or realise how seriously the position was looked upon by the locals. Family and I were ushered into the leading canoe of three and lead the way along the pristine river water powered by two Fijian paddle men in warrior garb, one front and one rear. 45 minutes of tough paddling later brought into sight a wooden jetty serving the village, crowded with villagers waving at the visitors. My canoe had been overtaken by the second in line which tried to make the jetty first but was turned away because the visiting chief was not aboard. I stepped on to the jetty, to be met by the village chief, who during the whole stay would not speak with anyone else but the visiting chief. The rest of the visitors were lined up behind me in single file by the village warriors, putting the men behind me, then the boys, then the women and finally the little girls, and we marched into the village in that order.

Seated aside, the village chief on ceremonial chairs, I and my tribe were welcomed to the village by the chief, to the warlike chanting of his warriors, which needed to be answered by the visiting chief, who couldn't raise a chant from his men and who didn't have a spear between them. It was all very gung ho, and me, being English was beginning to wonder if I should declare war and withdraw to the canoes to bring in reinforcements. The mood changed for the better when the village ladies started to sing traditional songs and clapped to their dancing. Then the chiefs were escorted to the largest hut where the feast was to be held, followed by the visitors still in single file, with the fearsome looking warriors ushering them along. I was silently hoping that I would not have to select one of my tribe for human sacrifice to celebrate the feast and thank the gods as we all sat on the floor of the hut around the banquet of local delicacies, much of which was unrecognisable as edible to me and my subjects.

Naturally, I was seated at the head of the spread next to the chief, and I could see my wife and grandsons way down the hut in their status place as it were. The chief spoke to me directly for the first time in fractured English telling me not to touch the food until his daughters arrived. The duty of the daughters when they did arrive was to feed the chiefs, everyone else had to feed themselves using fingers only. The cooked food was awful, but there was plenty of it, goodness knows what was eaten that day. The exception was the fruit which most diners favoured, and I had nothing to do but to allow food to be fed to me by the allotted daughter, who had a face like a rear end collision, and who I feared I might have to marry after the feast the way things were going. That fear was strengthened when the chief leaned over and said that he had chosen me to be the next village chief when he expired, which judging by his well-worn appearance wouldn't be many months away. Then the feast was cleared, and a large bowl was placed before me while still squatting next to the chief, and water, at least it looked like water was poured into it. Next, a bunch of what resembled hay was brought to the bowl by one of the daughters, who began dipping the hay into the water and wringing it out in a twisting action causing the water to turn a dirty brown. "Now time for cava," said the chief. I later discovered that cava was the Fijian hallucinogenic of choice, but as a coconut shell half filled with the dirty brown liquid was offered to me by the daughter, I politely refused to partake. This seemed to disappoint the chief who urged me to try it, which for the sake of not wanting to appear weak in front of my tribe, did so. It tasted vile, and I was pleased when it was passed around the sprawled out visitors, excepting the children of course. The bad news was that I was expected to drink the remains of the stuff when the shell was passed back to me. I sipped a little then returned it to the chief who drank the lot.

It must have had the desired effect because everyone started to dance to south sea music playing from speakers in the hut, and I was dragged on to the dance floor by the chief's number one daughter, which was probably expected by her father to honour the visiting chief. I eventually managed to shake off the daughter and join my family at the far end of the hut to my relief.

The single line was then reformed, and the party filed past the village craft stalls, then back down the jetty to board the canoes led by the two chiefs. The village chief then confiscated a packet of fine cigars, and a good lighter from my pockets then shook my hand vigorously before his retinue of warriors escorted him back to the village.

As the canoes paddled downstream, a gust of wind blew my sunhat into the river, and the cry went up from the Fijian paddlers, "The chief's hat is in the river turn around, turn around," which they did and rescued my hat from the transparent water. My two grandsons forever afterwards would ask me when I would be returning to the village to become chief. It would be injudicious to register my reply to the query.

Chapter Twenty-Two
All's Well That Ends Well
(1974)

The year was 1969, and my family and I had just begun an accrued extended leave having recently returned from three years overseas assignments in the Far East, ending in Sydney, Australia. I had lately been on secondment to the Indonesian branch to extend the factory premises in Jakarta and had arrived back in the UK via Sydney. The Manchester climate for all its reputation felt good after the oppressive climate endured in Indonesia in particular. There was, in fact, snow on the ground, a sight which our surprise house guest Fun had never seen before. Fun was the daughter of the Indonesian/Chinese building contractor, Suria Budiman, who had constructed the pharmaceutical factory I was contracted to build and commission. As was expected, Suria and his whole family turned up at the airport to bid farewell on completion of the contract, and it was at that moment that Suria took me aside and pushed $1000 into my hand, which was hurriedly returned with the comment that it couldn't be accepted as a gift. "No, no," said Suria. "This money is for you to accept my daughter into your home, and to support her and find her a good school in England." Taken aback, I was then introduced to 18-year-old Fun who did speak hesitant English and who promptly thanked me for taking her to England. Since this was the first time I had heard of the arrangement, I was dumbstruck to find that having arrived in Jakarta with two children, I would be returning to Manchester with three. Suria then apologised to me for not being able to get a ticket for Fun on the plane I was about to board a broad smile on his face assured me that she was booked to arrive in Manchester in two weeks' time. By this time, rushing to get my own luggage and family organised for boarding, I had no time to discuss the obvious ramifications of such an arrangement and was seated on the plane before I had time to think. "Do you think he was serious," said my wife?

"He sounded serious," I replied, "in any case we will find out in two weeks," as I recalled the money Suria had thrust into my pocket.

Following receipt of a telegram, I had collected Fun from Manchester airport and was now wondering what to do with her. I had little knowledge of suitable schools, and it was some time before I managed to enrol her into a Brighton based academy.

The outcome was that considering the little English she spoke, she worked tirelessly, eventually to attain a chartered architect status, now based in Newcastle, and although she never married, she maintains contact with our family though now nearing retirement herself as a British citizen.

Chapter Twenty-Three
How to Handle Australians
(1973)

For the past four or so, I had become somewhat accustomed to the idiosyncrasies of the oriental way of conducting business deals, also had developed a technique in the training of local staff to achieve acceptable levels of productivity. In all countries visited to date, I had encountered an overwhelming enthusiasm for learning from the locals, to the point of being pestered and questioned constantly, being expected to know everything ranging from organising administrative procedures to how to operate and repair high speed wrapping machines, to building and civil engineering standards. I had encountered untapped talent in all countries without which I could not have succeeded in my endeavours. I had found all this to be a rewarding experience, and when assigned to the Australian project, I naturally assumed that half the battle would have been fought by that time in terms of available talent and trades professionalism. It was there alright, but it was not available, there being a less than half a percent unemployment rate in the country—you couldn't get workers trained or untrained for love nor money.

I had empty factory space, all manufacturing equipment and ancillary plant delivered to site but no workers to install or operate any of it, plus a tight deadline to commence production to boot. My American employers had no ear for my plight, no excuses would be tolerated, do it or die was the order of the day. This was a totally different and unexpected challenge for me. I had been accustomed to an overflow of job applicants, but in Sydney, a developed economy, I got none. I advertised using all forms of media, contacting specialist agencies, but to no avail. In the first month, I had precisely three applicants, two of which were from outback hobos.

The U.S. Company I was contracted to did have an established associate company local to Sydney employing some 350 workers, and I reasoned that my only option was to 'borrow' some employees from them. They were anti this since they had the same problem in attracting staff, but after some often boisterous negotiations, I managed to pry 20 male workers away which was inadequate, but it was a start.

Slowly but slowly, the project made progress, and I had, by now, understood that previous training techniques were of no use to me, so I managed my small but growing team like a football team, which the locals understood. There were pommy insults flying around daily as I tried to harness my unruly mob into some sort of team, but it was very hard going, and many were the times that I had to draw on my mining engineering background to sort out the daily problems. The Aussies didn't take to being disciplined, and the only way I found effective was to do jobs myself if the men said it wasn't possible to do them. They hated being shown up which put a lot of pressure on me, but it was the only way, no other way stood a chance. Several workers fell by the wayside and returned to the associate company, but strangely enough, the word passed back by the workers who stayed, attracted increasing numbers to join my 'football team,' so much so that the associate company complained to their USA masters that I was committing daylight robbery of their employees and must be stopped. I now had, by fair means or foul, raised a team of some fifty tradesmen and somewhat behind schedule all plant and manufacturing machinery had been installed, ready for commissioning. The latter was going to prove to be the tricky part since female labour was required to operate the high speed wrapping and packing machines. How to find one hundred ladies was the toughest hurdle to surmount to date due to the full employment situation, and I knew that I could not pull the same trick again. I reasoned that I could not organise a ladies' football team using similar methods. The work being offered— manufacturing being a fast-moving consumer product—required a high level of dexterity which I as a male could not compete with the ladies, so doing it myself, though I tried, was not an option. I could, with help from my male workers, manufacture the product using the heavy equipment, but the wrapping and packaging required ladies skills. Desperate times call for desperate measures, and I hit on the idea of approaching the wives of the management officials of the associate company, plus my own wife, plus the wives of a few local friends. Using as much charm as I could muster and with some important input from my wife, I held an open day to demonstrate the manufacturing process from start to finish to a group of wives, most of whom were full time housewives. The demonstration captured the attention of a few of the ladies such that they became recruitment ambassadors, and within a week, I had a dozen ladies on my staff. Gradually, but too slowly to meet burgeoning sales, the product was launched and staff levels, although still too low, were improving.

The Aussies seemed to have an inbuilt dislike of anyone in authority, which I found difficult to deal with, particularly when trying to build a management and supervisory team. Struggling to meet the required productivity, on one occasion I called into my office Big John who was the supervisor of the manufacturing department and in no uncertain prose told him that productivity was too low and must be improved, setting him a realistic target for the following day. As I walked into my office at 9am, the following morning I was met by my secretary who urged me to go to the first aid room. Laid out on the black leather top of the examination bed was the prone body of the assistant manufacturing supervisor whose blood covered face was severely mangled. "Who did that?" I asked.

"John hit me," croaked the man, as he was wheeled away to the ambulance.

John stood before my desk with an implacable expression on his face, waiting to be congratulated on achieving his target for the first time. "You're fired John." John's face dropped and reddened.

"But I only did what you told me to do—get the target. The guy wouldn't do what I told him, so I hit him."

That was an understatement, because the man had been severely beaten in an act of rage. "I'm sorry John, but the company cannot condone violence of that nature—it is a dismissible offence." For one moment, I thought the big guy was going to drag me over my desk, but he just turned around and stormed out of the office.

Then there was Merve, the cleaner, a slightly built stooping chap in his fifties. On my morning inspection around the factory one early morning accompanied by the quality assurance manager, Rosie, I sniffed an unpleasant odour in a corridor adjacent to the sanitised production area. "Can you smell anything nasty Rosie?" I asked.

We both searched around to locate the foul odour permeating the corridor until I opened a broom cupboard to reveal row upon row of drying fish hanging by their pegged tails. The overpowering stench rushed out of the cupboard, causing us both to retreat hastily, our hands covering our noses. "Send Merve to my office," I blurted out from behind my cupped hand. The pathetic figure of Merve stood before the desk, reminding me that in Australia at that time, Merve was typical of the quality of casual labour available. Having reminded myself of this, I asked Merve whose fish was drying out in his air conditioned broom cupboard. "It's mine sir. I fish every morning before work, and the cupboard is grand for drying them out. I do take them home after work, so they won't smell." Lost for words, I read the riot act quietly to Merve regarding sanitised working environments, but the puzzled expression on the cleaner's face said that my words had fallen on stony ground

Without doubt, the Australian project was by far the toughest assignment in my much travelled career to date, and there was no question that without my early grounding in supervising the Lancashire miners, I would have stood no chance. I was therefore gratified to have made some lifelong friends from that country in addition to have left a successful operation behind me and counted having gained hard won respect from the Aussie team as my most gratifying achievement.

Chapter Twenty-Four
Good Morning, Mr Smith (1969)

I had finally arrived at the New Jersey headquarters for my first executive management meeting out of which my future with the company would be decided, having endured a harrowing taxi drive from New York through a metre of snow and arctic temperatures. I had just flown in to New York after an unbroken twenty two hour flight from Manila having been instructed to be present at 9am sharp on the Friday morning to attend a presentation by the CEO which 'you would be ill advised to miss' as the saying goes. My taxi rolled up to the office entrance at 8.50am, thanks to the driver's persistence and no mean skill in the treacherous conditions, warranting a hefty tip for his effort.

Needless to say, I didn't look or feel my best, unshaven and bedraggled would adequately describe my appearance—but I had made it, and I believed that the Americans never thought that I would, which gave me an incentive.

Seated at the large conference table, I couldn't recognise anyone I knew which was discomforting, but I put my briefcase on the table along with everyone else and took out the brief. That was the last thing I remembered doing before I felt my shoulders being gently shaken by the person seated next to me. I could faintly hear the presenter in the far distance who seemed not to notice that I was mentally absent. "So if we are serious about taking Smith Bros. into the group then I suggest we get a technical and financial viability study done ASAP. Who will be the responsible people for that?" I shook myself awake and noticed from the brief that I had been nominated to cover the technical aspect, so I raised a hand in acknowledgement along with two others. Presentation concluded, I collected my luggage from the foyer then made my way to the Governor Morris hotel and slept until Saturday morning.

The Monday morning car journey to Poughkeepsie in upstate New York, the home of the nationally famous Smith Bros. throat pastille, passed through wonderfully scenic countryside. Indian country was how my two American colleagues termed it, and nothing could have better described it, even though it was in its drab winter dress.

It was my first real perception of life outside metropolitan America, and I was looking forward to the experience. Poughkeepsie proved to be a quaint attractive little town by U.S. standards nestling in rolling hills, as the car rolled into the factory courtyard and we three stepped out to meet the president of the company, who must have spotted their arrival from his office window. The first thing which struck me was that he was dressed in Victorian fashion, the only item missing was his top hat.

He was reminiscent of a Quaker gentleman I mused, who I had met in the early days of my career years ago in Manchester, who dressed in much the same fashion.

Pleasantries and introductions were exchanged, and the president proved to be an extremely polite and welcoming gentleman who escorted us to his boardroom, where we all sat around a large splendid highly polished oval board table, surrounded by lavish panelled walls reminiscent of Victorian splendour. Before each of us on the table was placed the famous pocket sized tin of Smith's cough drops, hard boiled black pastille sized sweets which was the lifeblood of the old established company.

On the top panel of the tin were depicted Mr William and Mr Andrew Smith, the brotherly founders of the company, resplendent in Victorian dress complete with top hats. I developed the strangest feeling that we had entered an exhibition of Victoriana, particularly when I noticed that at one end of the long board room stood somewhat larger than life, cardboard cut outs of the two founding brothers leaning on their walking canes.

The business discussions however proceeded in anything but a Victorian manner. Hard facts referring to the proposed takeover covered the following two hours before it became time to tour the factory which was what I was there to assess. As we stood to don our protective white coats, the president escorted all three to stand before the cardboard cut-outs. "We need to pay our respects daily to Mr William and Mr Andrew before entering the factory. The staff and employees all say good morning to the effigies each day and good night when they leave, and I trust you will respect our tradition and follow suit while you are here." I had never spoken to a cardboard cut-out before and judging by the embarrassed expression on the faces of my two American colleagues, neither had they. "It is too late to say good morning now, but I would be pleased if you would kindly say to Mr William and Mr Andrew how pleased you are to be invited to enter the factory. Also, you will be here to say good evening when you leave for the day."

Monty Python made a fortune out of sketches like this I thought though I didn't mention that to my colleagues who probably wouldn't know who Monty Python was.

Quietly, I whispered to the two Americans that I would need to book myself an appointment to see my psychiatrist if I were to go through with the request, and there was no way I would be striking up a conversation with the card board effigies. Furthermore, it wasn't in my contract to do so. That triggered off one of the Americans into a giggling fit which started off the other. I kept my cool as best I could in what was a highly embarrassing incident in front of the bemused President, but it was no use, the damage was done, and the two gigglers had to retire to the restroom. The president then said to me that he respected my composed approach to the situation, which was probably due to the fact that I was English and understood what tradition was about. I acquiesced.

Without further insistence, I was ushered into the factory by the president since the two Americans had not returned and were not technical people anyway therefore were not really needed. What met my eyes took me aback—it was a Dickensian scene, right out of the Oliver Twist movie. I had expected an up to date at least semi-automated operation, but it was downright primitive by the standards of that day. It was patently obvious that the whole manufacturing process would require radical re investment, and the factory was massively overstaffed. Of course, I did not relay this to the president who greeted every worker with a smile and a kind word, and it was obvious that it must have been a pleasure to work there. I had my job to do, but it was clear that I could not recommend purchase of the business on purely technical grounds. Nevertheless, I was secretly pleased that within the savage world of dog eat dog in the takeover business that there were still islands the likes of Smith Brothers to maintain a modicum of sanity with maybe a little bit of insanity thrown in, even in the U.S.

Chapter Twenty-Five
Yes Sir, Yes Sir (1971)

Trying to get a telephone call through from Taiwan to New Jersey USA in 1971 was tantamount to getting a signal to Voyager 1 in today's world. It went via Australia to California then to New Jersey, and you found yourself talking to three or sometimes four international operators about the local weather or some other pleasant chatter before someone in the US office would say "Could you call me back please we seem to have a bad line", at which point the international operators would blame each other for the problem, and it was time for your lunch. Perseverance eventually paid off, and at least you felt more tolerant after lunch. I needed an expert high speed wrapping mechanic urgently to commission a critical production unit recently purchased from Japan which even the Japanese couldn't get to work, although it was a perfect copy of the American original.

Eugene had never been out of the States before, and when I greeted him at Taipei airport, he looked absolutely shattered and was in a terrible grumpy mood. Try as I may, I couldn't cheer him up even over dinner that evening, but allowances had to be made for the very long and tiresome journey he was unaccustomed to, and an early night was called for. However, the following morning, Eugene's mood had not changed one bit. Everything was wrong with the hotel, although at that time it was the best in town and would be classed four star even today.

It was obvious that Eugene thought that the rest of the world was to US standard and was not willing to compromise. Anyhow, I just needed his expertise to get the confounded machine to produce, and Eugene would just have to be tolerated to achieve that end.

Although Eugene was but 5ft 3inches tall, he possessed an aggressive nature with a voice to match, and I was concerned as to how the Chinese operatives would take to his training approach, particularly since they did not speak English and an interpreter would be required. It was a disaster, but within a few days, Eugene had at least got the machine to work, however, the Chinese remained baffled. Eugene had dispensed with the interpreter and obviously thought that if he got angry and shouted at the operators loud enough in English, they would understand him. Strangely enough, the Chinese found him funny and would outrage him by smiling and occasionally laughing and bowing repeating "yes sir, yes sir" as he ranted at them in sometimes fruity language. They took no offence at all and always greeted him with respect, but Eugene could not understand his inability to upset them, and I had to step in to cool the situation regularly as Eugene got beside himself in frustration.

By the end of the week, the operators having probably taught themselves how to master the machine, said good bye to Eugene who still couldn't understand the respect they showed him. He certainly had little respect for them when recording his trip report to me, who had the doubtful pleasure of taking Eugene to a good restaurant for a farewell dinner. The rainy season had begun, and heavy tropical rains were a daily event. So, it was the evening of the dinner, and Eugene was scathing about the weather and the hotel and just about everything else during the meal. As we left the restaurant, my driver met us with a large umbrella and all dashed to the car in torrential rain. Eugene preferred to sit beside the driver with myself and my wife in the rear. Eugene was waxing lyrical about life in the States as the car drew up in front of the Ambassador hotel and the doorman ran to the car door holding an umbrella. Out stepped Eugene and promptly disappeared into a fast flowing open drain where the concrete cover slab was missing. He was clinging to the next downstream slab for dear life, trying to stop himself from being swept away down the 3feet deep 2feet wide drain which was a torrent. I dashed from the car in the pouring rain as did my driver, and together with the doorman we managed, with some effort, to drag him from the drain and lay him on the forecourt. He would certainly have drowned had he been swept away since all the heavy concrete covers were in place downstream, and the water filled the depth of the culvert.

So ended Eugene's first and last trip overseas. My driver must have relayed the incident to the factory operators because they smiled and bowed at me when I went to the machine the following morning, making me wonder which Chinese proverb had been vetted.

Chapter Twenty-Six
The Skateboard Waltz (1974)

The docks at Tanjun Priok Djakarta Indonesia was not the place to be, after dark in particular, or indeed at all, except, of course, if you were fortunate enough to be invited for evening dinner at the locally famous sea food restaurant, where the ambience was unsurpassed, and the quality and variety of seafood was indescribable, and well worth the risk to life and limb from the dock thugs. Wives had to be kept under close surveillance at all times, and this had been carefully explained to myself and wife who were newcomers to the group. To include a couple of Australian heavies in the eight strong group was just common sense and had already been taken care of. They did inform me that the heavies had been working out the week before, although I dismissed this as Aussie talk, but hoped it was true having heard some of the stories emanating from previous excursions, which I had seen fit not to relate to my wife.

Just to take the risk to go there just for a meal must mean that the experience had got to be worth it, and I thought that if the Aussies, (plus one German and one American couple) could do it then I was not about to let the side down. Mind you, the American (ex Guyana) lady was enough to frighten anybody.

It was tradition that evenings out at Tanjun Priok were timed to have dinner finished by 8pm, then a quick dash to the cars if they were still there, then home by 8:30pm or so for after dinner drinks in the relative safety of someone's home. The trip recorded here went horribly wrong in that when the party reached the restaurant, they discovered that it had been commandeered by Indonesian government officials despite the reservation made by the ex pat party. We were met by a member of staff, recognisable by his filthy and stained white apron who entreated the party to wait a short while until the Very Impertinent Persons had left. They had apparently descended on the restaurant unannounced and pulled rank but had been there since lunchtime and were too drunk to remember who they were. One by one, the officials staggered out of the door in a most undignified manner until order was restored, but the party would now not finish their meal until 9:30 or even later. This was a serious concern since at 9pm the night clubs in the vicinity opened for business, and all the knives would have been sharpened by then. The consensus came out in favour of having our meal but to urge the restaurant staff to serve us as quickly as possible.

To describe the interior of the restaurant as being basic would be rating it too highly. Peeling multi-coloured paint, long refectory like thick topped scrubbed wooden tables with wooden benches down each side, all being scrubbed by staff to remove the awful mess left by the VIPs. The stench of wet wood combined with the odour from the huge cast iron cooking vat sitting on a bonfire at one end of the room was overpowering. The vessel was full of madly boiling water spitting in every direction and was not too far from the end of the table occupied by the party. The head cook was a Chinese national surrounded by three of four mini cooks of local origin. A portly man, he was wearing a filthy 'white' tee shirt with matching filthy apron, but he had a dazzling white toothed smile which he directed at his customers. He turned around and marched to the rear of the café and returned carrying a large bowl overflowing with a myriad of sea food, and with assistance from his assistants, he threw the contents of the bowl into the boiling water. The cooks then surrounded the vessel brandishing long poled whatnots, and what they did was unseen, but very soon, they marched to the newly scrubbed table and simply tipped the lot out into a large wicker shallow concaved basket when it was every man for himself. There were whole crabs and lobsters, squids, abalone, and octopus, plus any other crustaceans you could imagine. Implements to assist dissection were strewn across the table, grab them if you can, was the order of the day, and it was all quite primitive—but the culinary experience and sheer quality of the fare was quite exceptional. As the basket neared empty, another refill was signalled to the beaming chef by beckoning, and he would oblige. Beer was provided all for a set tariff, and the whole evening was reminiscent of a rowdy evening at a docks tavern in the days of long John Silver.

It was after 10pm, way beyond witching hour, when, not to follow the example of our V.I.P betters, we attempted a dignified departure. I was the only one almost fit to drive, the other men having to rely on their merry spouses as the group tried to organise themselves into some kind of civilised order. The order was shouted 'stick together' as we moved gingerly in the dark through the night club district en route to our parked cars. Men at the front and rear, ladies in between. I was with the leading men when, in the darkness, we stumbled through a curtain made from sackcloth and found ourselves in a night club of sorts. It was no more than a large shed, almost unlit, music playing, and there was a peculiar odour wafting around. It was very dark except for a faint violet glow, when suddenly realising our predicament, the men pushed back to keep the others from entering. I then heard a faint female voice say, "Dance please." This was repeated twice more, but I could see no one before me when someone pulled my trousers at the knee. Looking down, I could just make out a girl, but she was legless, and her torso was strapped to a square board with castors at each corner. Shocked at the sight, I forced the group behind me out of the place, and we all beat a hurried retreat to our vehicles which were fortunately still there. The whole episode was reminiscent in my mind to dockside films he had seen in my 1950s youth starring Humphrey Bogart and Peter Lorre.

The previous night out at Tanjun Priok troubled me on my way into work the following morning, in particular the obscene sight of the skateboard girl, but as I approached a busy traffic light controlled junction on the main dual carriage roadway through the city, the lights changed to red, and I stopped, only to witness an even more sickening sight. I was accustomed to being accosted at traffic lights by beggars, usually children pressed into service, but on that morning, the beggars at the lights were horribly disabled children with twisted limbs, unable to stand. Just then, marching through the line of cars, came a man who collected the four boys by lifting them one by one off the ground by the pants belt, much like a suitcase and carrying them away, obviously at the end of their shift. The rough way he grabbed them swinging them as he walked was truly a sickening sight, and a disturbing memory.

The answer to your question is "No. You never get used to it."

Chapter Twenty-Seven
Where Is the Runway? (1985)

It was my first visit to the Santa Cruz California factory, in fact to anywhere near California including San Francisco. I was seconded there to see how things were done by beings from the future, and I was certainly hoping to add to my already comprehensive experience of the business. Notwithstanding this, I was always receptive to improving my store of knowledge, and where better to do that than the sunshine state. Being accommodated at the aptly named Dream Inn located on the beach seemed pertinent to what I expected, judging by the stories told to me by head office management. I got a flavour of what I was told to expect when on the second morning into work, my taxi was halted for twenty minutes or so at a traffic light by the car driver in front being threatened by a gun wielding hobo. The police dragged him away following a struggle, but I gave generously after that.

I was assigned a minder following that incident, a six foot raw boned tough looking cowboy complete with Stetson and boots—no side arms but what he carried inside his shirt looked highly suspicious. He worked in the factory which was his day job, and only converted to his cowboy outfit at 5pm after work, when he assumed his minder duties. I took an instant liking to the easy going style of Kyle who had been raised on the board walk, and who promised to show me what living on the board walk was really like. Having Kyle around certainly gave me an enhanced feeling of security as I was shown around the dockside and introduced to every trawler skipper there by my minder who everybody seemed to know and respect.

The board walk was his home and upbringing, and the funfair owners who were his family and friends were truly fascinating people. I likened them to the English gypsy folks, colourful mobile homes and cabins, and they found my accent and English manners intriguing as they quizzed me about life in the outside world.

I listened with interest to their stories which were told around the dinner table and was appreciative of the down to earth welcome I received from these often maligned folks.

At the other end of the scale were the super neurotic types I encountered in San Francisco. Lovely and interesting town, but there are for sure some weird people walking the streets there—or maybe I was expecting too much. While waiting in the queue at the tramcar terminus together with my Japanese host for the day, I was, for no particular reason, accosted by a bible thumping loud mouthed man dressed in something he could have only hired for the day. "Did you have sex before marriage?" he shouted in my face.

"Why of course," I replied instantly, "didn't you?" The holy man then condemned me to everlasting damnation, and the queue erupted in laughter. Adjacent to the queue was a large shop window selling marital aids, none of which were recognisable to me. In fact, I initially thought they were selling instruments of torture until my host corrected me. There were people skateboarding all over the place, on the pavements, crossing the road dangerously between cars, some even dressed normally carrying briefcases or shopping items. It occurred to me that these people had arrived on the west coast in covered wagons as pioneers. What happened?

My Japanese host, suggested that I see the more refined side of the West Coast and drove me to Carmel, home of the stars so I was told. What a contrast! I loved the place—sophisticated and stylish with an English market town feel about it, expensive but worth it. I had a beer in Clint Eastwood's Hogs Breath pub before I was driven to San Francisco airport to board a Philippine Airlines flight to Sydney Australia to visit the company factory there en route to the UK.

The Boeing 707 was seven hours into the 15 hour flight over the Pacific when the pilot announced to the passengers that the plane was running out of fuel and that they had sent out a distress signal to that effect. This announcement had a profound impact on the ladies on board, some screamed some shouted at the hostesses who did their best to quieten things down. The good news then announced by the captain was that the plane was not leaking fuel but that the airport staff had not filled the tanks sufficiently to make the 15 hour flight You may ask why someone in the cockpit hadn't noticed that before they took off, but the captain was not taking questions. Having exonerated himself from blame probably to ensure continued pension payments to his family, he later made the announcement which soothed passengers' anxiety somewhat. The nearest source of fuel was Wake Island, the U.S. air force base which was four hours flight time away on the western side of the Pacific from where the 707 was, and he believed that he had sufficient fuel to reach Wake. The nervous tension among the passengers was obvious as the plane banked sharply to the right and set course for Wake Island.

Wake Island is no tourist destination. As the plane descended for landing, I could see nothing but water. Lower and lower until the undercarriage must hit the water so close was it. Where was the runway? It seemed an age before a narrow strip of sand appeared under the plane then tarmac, and the plane wheels hit terra firma with a hell of a bump. Reverse thrust immediately as the pilot tried valiantly to bring the plane to a halt which he finally managed to do. Wake was no more than a fuel pump, a few vehicles and a large Nissan hut plus some scattered outbuildings nearby. What a desolate posting for the ground staff, though I knew that it played a vital strategic role for the U.S. during the World War Two Pacific campaign although it is but a tiny atoll poking above the waves. Not that the passengers on the plane were about to cast any aspersions about the place as they witnessed the fuel tanker topping up their tanks. It was certainly a mood changer.

Chapter Twenty-Eight
Goodbye Gladys (1970)

By a sheer stroke of good fortune, my wife was invited to a coffee morning by a close friend to be held at St Christopher's Catholic Church in Taipei which was the church we attended during our stay in Taiwan. Not being a coffee morning addict, she hesitated to accept but did so in deference to her friend and was certainly pleased that she did, for she was further invited to attend an address to the community on a following evening to be given by no less than the highly respected missionary Gladys Aylward—the 'little woman' as she was fondly referred to, whose gallantry and dedication to her Chinese flock is well documented in books and film.

On returning from the evening of the Aylward address, June was overcome by the passion and power of the 'little woman' and said that she had been emotionally drained by the sincerity, honesty and compassion evident in the inspirational exhortation, which pulled no punches in relation to criticism of the Chinese government in office at that time. June was particularly surprised by the power and command of oratory emitting from such a tiny lady.

As events turned out, it was Gladys' last sermon for she unexpectedly died a few days later from pneumonia. The whole island was in shock at her sudden demise, for she was held as an icon by not only the grown up children she had saved in her epic trek from the mainland but by all the Chinese people. Crowds of people both Chinese and the foreign ex pat community turned out in force to walk behind her cortege through the city centre brandishing placards showing photographs, also Chinese character and English messages of salutation giving testament to the love and respect they had for the tiny missionary. June and I managed to be quite close to the vehicle carrying the coffin, but the vehicle itself could not be seen because it was covered entirely in flowers even concealing the wheels. How the driver could see where he was going was a mystery as he inched his way up the mountain slopes of Yang Min Shan in pouring monsoon rain. Part way up the mountain, the cortege made a short diversion to a spot which overlooked the sea towards mainland China and selected Chinese, probably from amongst the hoard of children she battled to save all those years ago carried the flower bedecked coffin to the open grave. June and I were close enough to see the coffin lowered but we were dismayed to see that the grave was full to the brim with rainwater. That didn't seem to deter the coffin bearers as they placed the coffin adjacent to the watery grave. We thought it was, as did most of the foreign community, a rather undignified end for a very dignified lady, but maybe local custom dictated.

We trudged away leaving tearful Chinese standing at the graveside in the easing rain preferring not to witness the lowering of the coffin.

Chapter Twenty-Nine
Knock It Down (1979)

Together with family, I arrived at a rain-swept Taipei airport to a bumpy and unnerving landing in total darkness, weary from the 15 hour journey. Despite the lateness of the hour, the Taiwanese customs insisted on searching through every item of our voluminous luggage since we had arrived via Hong Kong, despite being told that Hong Kong was our transit stop. We later discovered that they treated every traveller who arrived via Hong Kong with the same diligence, and since the vast majority of flights into Taipei in those days arrived via the shoppers' paradise the customs officers enjoying rich pickings from the unwary. Cleared at last, we dragged our ravaged luggage and two chirpy children to the taxi rank where I bargained for a taxi to the hotel and was pleased to be told that I had only paid twice the going rate for the ride. As we entered our room, the telephone rang. Wondering who would be ringing me at such a late hour in a country where I knew no one, I picked up the handset, and a lady's voice said, "Can I come up now captain?" Puzzled at my promotion, I replaced the handset. My wife enquired who rang.

"No idea," I replied, "but I've been promoted". Within three weeks following our arrival, we had found an English speaking school run by Dominican nuns incorporating lay teachers, also importantly a sturdily built house way up the Shan overlooking Taipei situated on the Methodist theological college campus, which appeared to be a secure location to our inexperienced eyes. As Catholics, we were the only non-Methodists on the campus but that did not exclude us from the regular door to door collections supporting Methodist causes.

It was on my first day in the Taipei city office that I met Robert Sih who had bid for the factory construction contract, hence the comprehensive folio which I had carried from the US, and a hefty file it was, as I recall, sturdily bound and of considerable weight. It was itemised down to the last screw, a masterpiece of detail. To add to the proliferation of terms was the fact that the whole contract document was translated into Chinese at the rear of the folio, which had to be read from the back page to first page and each page read from right to left— English, in front of the folio, read from front page to back page, and from left to right. Robert spoke halting English, I spoke no Chinese. I struggled manfully to explain our requirements under the terms of the contract, whipping pages backwards and forwards to show him the translations, but after half an hour, Robert burst into laughter and threw his hands in the air in defeat. "This my number one factory for 'foreign,' I do everything you want, anything no problem for me, I sign anything." With that, we signed and countersigned. Robert hence forth proved to be truer to his oath than any one I have ever met in business. He was a unique individual, and from start to finish we retained mutual respect for each other, he was a joy to work with over the three year project.

Robert was an irrepressible character working from dawn to dusk, determined to make a success of his first foreign contract which in those early days in Taiwan's industrialisation would considerably enhance his reputation on the island, and in addition bolster his chances of successful tendering for other foreign contracts in the escalating 'invasion' by particularly USA and European multinationals. The next day, Robert drove me 30 miles down island to the small town of Neili to view the industrial development area designated for factory construction which to my surprise was an inundated area of rice paddy fields. This explained why we had purchased two pairs of Wellington boots en route out of the city. There was, however, a sealed roadway snaking through the water logged fields, and I could see three construction sites in progress around the perimeter. Our site was virgin paddy field, and as I stood ankle deep in the water and rice shoots clutching the contract folio, I posed the obvious first question to Robert. How long to drain the paddy and fence our perimeter. Robert was just five feet three inches tall and was entrenched deeper into the mud than I was. He looked up at me and uttered for the first time the phrase I was to hear regularly over the next three years. "No ploblem, sir." Within the next two weeks, he had the site clear of water and securely fenced and gated.

Meanwhile, I was required to personally attend the Taiwan income tax office to register my income for PAYE and did so with trepidation having heard one or two ex pat stories of long waits and aggressive questioning by officials. The revenue officers were enclosed behind a solid wooden divider running the length of the room with a series of small hatches along its length with vertical sliding closures. Victims were required to sit on wooden benches to await their call as a hatch slide would be suddenly raised and a voice would shout a surname which would often be ignored by the customers due to garbled pronunciation by the Chinese staff trying to get their tongue around the variety of western surnames. I ignored mine at least three times before the repetitive voice of the caller reached soprano level. When I reached the open hatch, I found that the hatch opening was level with my chest, and I was almost bent double trying to talk to the inscrutable face peering at me. Of course, I had brought proof of my terms of contract from Warner Lambert Inc. to substantiate my claims, but the officer was not in the least interested and pushed the documents back at me when I tried to present them. He then asked me for the nationality of my company and what position I held with them, then referred to a large book and told me what my salary was, which was twice what it actually was. I started to object in earnest when he advised me of my monthly tax liability which equalled my actual salary. Interview over— the hatch door slammed down, and I stretched my aching back to stand upright. Somewhat in mild shock, I sent an urgent telex to home base in New Jersey explaining the situation and requesting that my salary be increased to cater for the swinging tax deduction. An interchange of interesting telexes later, the increase was agreed just in time for the first end of month salary payments, otherwise it could have been a very short stay.

A company car was delivered to my mountain home, a Nissan Cedric assembled in Taiwan which considerably improved family mobility, although buses trains and taxis were relatively cheap and plentiful. The car was large and comfortable, but all the handles and control knobs kept falling off. I would wait until several had dropped off before taking it back to the garage to refit, and this continued for the three years I had the car. They just could not get the pesky things to stay on. I would be winding down a window and the handle would come off in my hand, otherwise the car was fine. As I mentioned beforehand, these were early days in the country's emergence, and patience and understanding was called for, otherwise you could become a nervous wreck in short time. Signs of the boom to come were evident all around, and the hard working locals were busy all the time. Never did you see anyone strolling or lounging on street corners, everyone was doing something. I was fully occupied spending the majority of my time in the city office on placing orders for equipment and materials and recruiting city office management staff, finding time only to visit the construction site one day per week, relying on Robert to carry out my instructions week by week.

On my first visit to the appointed company lawyer to clarify complicated Taiwanese import licensing regulations, I was thwarted as his secretary escorted me into his office to see Mr Lee disappearing through his sixth floor window. His driver standing in the yard below saw him falling and bravely tried to catch him with disastrous consequences for them both. Mr Lee was killed, and his driver critically injured. This was, apart from the personal tragedy for Mr Lee's family, a blow for many of the foreign investors to the island since Mr Lee was the most respected and influential business lawyer on the island at that time. He was replaced by his son of the same name who eventually re-established his father's reputation for the practice.

I was requested to attend the office of the import licencing authority to explain why the company was contravening the import licence regulations set by the government of the Republic of China as Taiwan was officially called in those days. Great care had to be taken with importation documents since the authorities were sticklers for accuracy, and I assumed that would be the reason for my summons. On my arrival, I was shown a pro forma invoice, and a bill of lading which the official said showed that we were importing different food flavours than the licence authorised. Despite my assurances that we were not, this fell on deaf ears. "You see clearly sir that the licence approval says orange oil, peppermint oil, etcetera," said the officer, "but the bill of landing shows oil of orange, oil of peppermint and so on. This is different material, and you cannot clear through customs, it will be confiscated." I stifled a laugh but tried to appear inscrutable and remain composed as I again tried to explain that the materials were the same but to no avail. I was advised that the only way to clear the flavours was to provide proof that one was the same as the other. I racked my brain as to how to achieve that and came up with the idea that an explanatory telex from the supplier might do the trick. The supplier must have thought me crazy when they received my telex which read: 'Please send telex to me stating exactly the following wording. Oil of orange is orange oil, oil of peppermint is peppermint oil etc.' It worked, and I got my flavours.

I well recall the first time I drove myself to the factory site at Neili. I had been pre warned about the hazards and been advised to hire a driver which I did eventually, but meanwhile I braved the journey despite the bodies by the roadside, the myriad of scooters and small motorbikes, and worst of all the completely crazy pig truck drivers. These drivers had scant regard for any other vehicle as they dashed to the abattoirs, occasionally stopping to slosh paddy field water over the cruelly packed load of live pigs to cool them down and retain their body weight to fetch the maximum price at auction. The deafening squealing of the animals was a testament to their inhuman crushing into the wire mesh cages. These drivers were responsible for the majority of the roadside bodies, primarily scooter and motorbike riders which they treated as fodder, and if you saw one coming in your rear view mirror or from the opposite direction, it was wise to pull off the two lane highway and give him a wide berth. The road trip was so life threatening that even when I did hire a driver, I graduated to the reliable train journey for safety reasons and allowed driver Chen to ferry my wife around as gradually I was required to be at the factory site full time.

Robert provided me with a site cabin, and I travelled routinely Monday to Thursday to Neili, spending Friday in the Taipei office. Thus began the daily site inspections as I would accompany Robert around the site where he would proudly describe the progress being made. It should be made clear that Robert was not technically trained or qualified in the arts of construction, but what he lacked in that regard he made up for in intelligence and sheer determination to succeed, in addition to his willingness to learn and correct his mistakes as he went along. That was where I came in. Robert thought that I knew everything which is a heavy burden to bear, but he would always take advice when given. His work crew on the other hand were skilled in their various trades which was a bonus. On occasions, Robert would show me some construction that my expression would convey to him dissatisfaction with the quality of the work. I had, on previous occasions, taught him the expression 'knock it down,' and by now he would read my facial signal that all was not to my liking, then he would look up at me with a wry expression and say, "Knock it down?" before I could say it. At the eventual hand over of the completed factory, Robert maintained that he had built the factory twice over and had made no money on the project but was nevertheless more than happy with the reputation he had achieved amongst the island's business community.

Sitting in my cabin on one occasion, I was surprised when the door burst open, and Robert dashed in to tell me that one of his workers had fallen into the large open fronted concrete mixer while tipping in material from a loading ramp. Robert was obviously shaken by the incident but pulled himself together saying that I should not worry because he had already offered the man a job as a watchman which he could do successfully even with one arm.

As a contrast, we received visit from the USA head office Director of International Projects who was country hopping arriving from Hong Kong and who had stayed at the Hong Kong Hilton hotel. He had been impressed by the design of the concrete block sun screen fronting the hotel and instructed me to ignore the designed screen for our factory and go to the Hong Kong Hilton to study their design and replicate it. This I did, but as I was standing outside the Hilton, I got some strange looks from the hotel doormen as I measured and sketched the concrete blocks of the sun screen façade. Back in Taiwan, Robert and I put our heads together and eventually managed to design a casting mould for the quite complicated block, which was designed specifically for the Hilton hotel in that at the rising and the setting of the sun, the faceted blocks would shade to show a thousand H outlines over the full frontage. I expect it still does so. "Can you manufacture these Robert?" Of the many concrete sun screens in Taiwan at the time, none matched the complexity of the Hilton block, but Robert was not fazed by that, providing that I issued him with a variation to contract order.

"Agreed." Two weeks elapsed before I was presented with a sample block and a doubled price to go with it. "Agreed and well done Robert." Robert beamed at the compliment. Disaster struck however when the truck driver delivering the load of blocks to the site tipped them in a heap and broke the lot. It was Robert's own transport company who made the delivery, and he was furious, although it was all shouted in Chinese, and I wasn't sure if there was going to be a summary execution or not such was the furore.

Shortly following the blocks saga, I left Taiwan for four weeks home leave, Robert having assured me that he would replace the screen blocks and added that he hoped to have the screen built before my return. As I arrived back at the factory site and seated in the taxi, I could see from the roadside that the frontage sun screen was erected and gleaming bright white in the morning sun. It looked dazzling. Robert met me as I stepped out of the car, his chest swelled with pride and his beaming smile said it all. He ushered me to view the façade full frontage, and it was then that I noticed that the screen structure was not vertical but leaning to the right by a few degrees. This gave the impression that the whole factory was leaning. I was not looking forward to telling Robert this, so instinctively, I picked up a large concrete building block as Robert watched in wonder. I placed my left foot on the block with my right on the ground which obviously put me at an angle as I viewed the factory front. Then I stepped off the block and invited Robert to repeat what I had just done. He looked at me curiously but put his left foot on the block and looked at the sun screen. His eyes closed slowly, and I could swear that I saw a tear as he realised what I was demonstrating. Truthfully, he turned his head while still standing on the block and whimpered, "Knock it down?" I nodded ruefully.

The large concrete water storage tank on the roof was rebuilt three times before it would hold water, and Robert was at pains to point to this eventual success. Then he sprung a surprise by pointing out that he had completed the tarmacked road to the rear of the factory while I was away which was last on the schedule to be completed, which meant that the construction as a whole was complete. We strolled around to the back of the factory on the shiny new black tarmac to find that the road had been inclined such that it ended at the shipment store floor level and we walked straight in. A little bell rang in my head recalling that the plan called for the store floor to be some three feet above road level to enable loaded fork lifts to run straight into the road trucks. Sad to say I was right, but this time it was 'dig it up' not 'knock it down' which although improving Robert's grasp of English did little to cheer him up. Not to worry, Robert cheerfully called in the diggers and re-laid the whole road.

Occasionally, Robert would invite myself and my wife to dinner in one the many excellent Chinese restaurants in Taipei together with his charming wife Anna, who was obviously of northern Chinese origin being a little taller than Robert, with slim facial features, and very reserved in nature. She spoke English quite well and was pleasant company, with a sense of humour and appeared to be a perfect foil for Robert's ebullient outgoing manner. Over dinner on one occasion, I asked Robert how he came to Taiwan all those years ago, since he had told me previously that Shanghai was his hometown. It was a tale of heroism on Robert's part, and he was hesitant in the presence of the ladies to tell of the full horror of those days which he did tell me later. He was a boy of ten when Mao's communists rampaged into Shanghai in 1949, forcing large sections of the population to flee. In the turmoil that followed, Robert became separated from his parents and on his own initiative ran through the streets to the docks where the refugees had crowded on to any available boat they could find. When he arrived at the docks, all the boats had set sail except one lone tramp steamer which had just moved away from its mooring and was pulling away from the dock. Robert noticed that there were ropes trailing in the water from the stern of the steamer and dived in, then managed to grab one of the ropes. After being towed for a while, he managed to climb vertically up the rope until he was dragged on board by the scruff of the neck.

At a later dinner date, Robert brought along an American couple who he introduced to my wife and I as prospective clients of his who had requested Robert to quote for the construction of a factory to produce fishing flies for the American market. The owner of the business apparently was the husband's father who had cornered the fishing flies market in the US and was looking to expand his market overseas. Dinner was progressing during which the American who was well over six feet tall and heavily built became increasingly abusive to his wife for no apparent reason to the point where it was becoming embarrassing to the rest of us and the tables around. Robert tried to quieten the man by asking him nicely to refrain from talking to his wife in an insulting fashion but to no avail. Then the man's wife who had not in any way retaliated, started to shed tears at which point Robert jumped out of his chair, pulled himself up to his full five feet three and tore off his jacket then clenching his fists he thrust them into the face of the spoiled child and shouted, "If you want to fight, fight me, come outside, I fight you." I grabbed one of Robert's muscular arms as he was raring to go, but the situation resolved itself when the big American, who was obviously taken aback at the challenge, fled to the street dragging his unfortunate wife with him.

Robert shouted after him, "I no build you a factory, go home." The rest of the restaurant cliental had stopped eating to watch the shindig, but there were smiles and claps all around. Robert calmed down and apologised to me and my wife, but I said that there was no need to apologise and told him that he had gone up in my estimation which he didn't understand, but he got the message judging by the beaming smile he gave me.

The factory at Neili had reached the stage where I was ready to hire factory management and operatives. Although the competition for skilled workers amongst the relatively few foreign companies was keen, in particular supervisory and management staff, there were abundant applications to my advertisements. There was local university graduates available, and I knew that the work ethic amongst the Chinese was high, which was a head start. I needed a right hand man, a factory manager who could be relied upon to guide me through the mysteries of local industrial law and work customs. The factory being situated in a relatively rural area didn't help for I was surrounded by rice and livestock farmers, but there were a few local engineering establishments repairing anything from bicycles to motor cars, plus several Chinese craft workshops producing all manner of goods. I was fortunate in selecting John Chiang from my list of candidates for the factory manager position, for he proved to be a gem. A Christian university qualified engineer, although with little work experience, he proved to be an honest hard working individual who was respected by all factory staff and operatives. Eventually, we were fully staffed with the exception of a very high speed wrapping machine mechanic, a very specialised and important individual, who would be responsible for the training of other mechanics in that trade. There was just no one available except myself who had limited practical skills in the maintenance of high speed machines and try as we may even, John Chiang couldn't conjure up a candidate, so in order to commence production, I had to stand in which interfered radically with my own daily routine. Then three months into operation, I received word from John that there was an outstanding practical engineer working for an adjacent farmer repairing his tractor and other farm implements, and would I like to interview him. It was grasping at straws since the man I was told had no basic education at all and further was told that his farmer master owned him. Apparently, this meant that the farmer provided him with a straw bed in a barn on the farm plus two rice meals per day and gave him the equivalent of twenty five pence UK per week. Furthermore, if I wanted to interview him, I would have to do so at 10pm or later in the evening when he was able to slip away from his master to meet me in a neighbouring field. John said that if his master discovered what the man was up to, he could be severely beaten or worse. It was certainly the strangest interview I have ever conducted. John and I, at close to midnight, in a rice field interviewing a candidate by torchlight, he on one side of a hedgerow and me on the other side. The man was literally dressed in rags, and my first impressions were not good. He spoke no English at all, and John said that he only spoke an indigenous Taiwanese dialect but assured me that in the area he was a highly regarded craftsman. I took a chance and through John offered him a job, with a wage and conditions that were out of his realm of expectation. John then sprung another surprise. Would I give him a name because he didn't have one? "Tom," I said. John told him his name, and his face lit up with a smile and he nodded. Tom told us that he could not promise to turn up on the date we asked him to because his master watched him carefully, and he would have to plan his escape. Also, he was nervous about his suitability to work for a foreign company saying that he had only known his master who 'secured' him as a young boy, and if he failed to make the standard we required, he would be in a desperate state. I could read the fright in his eyes and yet he had the aura of honesty about him, and through John, I assured him that we would continue to employ him in some capacity if he did not make the grade with the high speed machines. Tom agreed that he would turn up at the factory but couldn't promise a fixed date, but he would do his best, and we had to leave it at that. John and I made our way through the paddy fields by torchlight to the roadside where my driver Chen was waiting.

I was seated at my desk at the factory one morning when my secretary came in to tell me that I had a visitor. But not the kind of business visitor I usually got selling his wares. She seemed a little embarrassed when I asked her who it was, and she just put her hands together in prayer. Intrigued, I asked her to show him in which she did. It was an old monk in his flowing colourful robes accompanied by a man in western dress. The latter spoke politely to me in English saying that the factory was welcome in his town of which he was mayor, then introduced his companion not as a monk but as the 'grand master of the 'Society of Dragons' He then went on to say that he was disappointed to have to tell me that the factory would pass through bad times because I had not had the opening blessed by the Dragon Master. I must admit that I had never given that a thought. The old 'monk' looked at me through his red makeup and put on his inscrutable look of foreboding. Luckily for me, the mayor went on, all things could be rectified by holding a Dragon Dance of reconciliation which he assured me would grant me full dispensation for my unforgiveable error. What could I do but agree. The 'dance' would take two hours to perform, and the factory would have to close production during the ceremony which I wasn't too pleased about and suggested that Saturday morning would be a good time for me.

"Dragons don't work Saturdays," said the mayor and in any event all the factory operators had to be present. How would tomorrow morning suit you said the mayor. I agreed providing that the performers could start at 8:00am since we had trucks arriving and departing from 10:00am onwards, and they would require the front entrance to be clear for that time. The mayor looked at the twitching face of the chief dragon who was contemplating the early start, but we both knew that there was money at stake here, and I was on the point of telling him the story of St George when he gave a reluctant nod. I arrived prompt at 7:30am the following morning to find the area in front of the factory swarming with people setting up stage props depicting dragons and mythical creatures, and laid out on the grass lawn was the very long dragon, huge head and lifeless. I went into my office, and John was organizing the whole company workforce outside surrounding the dragon. Spot on 8am, for the Taiwanese were always prompt with their timing, I was requested to stand at the top of the steps at the entrance door to witness the performance. My secretary stood beside me because she had the brown envelopes containing money taken from the daily cash float. I never did check the daily cash reconciliation afterwards, so I don't know how it was recorded. Maybe under Dragon. The lifeless dragon on the lawn suddenly came alive as the dancers whirled in a maniacal circle, the humps of its back rising and falling to the beat and sounds of drums and Chinese flutes. Every now and then, it would pause when the head was in front of me, and its huge mouth would open and come up close to my face. The only way I could appease the beast was to place a brown envelope on to its large red tongue, the mouth closed and off it went again on its mad swirling. I couldn't help but to be impressed by the stamina and strength of the men under the dragon, and I did notice that they had substitutes laying on the grass as one would roll from under the dragon another would take his place—very professionally done. There couldn't have been many company executives around the world that day who began their day by feeding a dragon. You can get rid of a lot of brown envelopes in two hours believe me, and we had to occasionally resort to the cash safe to keep up with the dragons' appetite. I was given a certificate to display on our noticeboard that we had appeased the dragon god and that good luck would befall the factory and its workers. That certificate was put to the test quite soon afterwards when I was atop the flat roof of the building inspecting Robert's ever leaking water storage tank and his latest attempt to stem the leak. The sky went dark as an ominous black cloud rolled across the sky until dusk descended at midday, but the rain held off, and there was an eerie charged atmosphere all around. I well recall the spookiness which had very quickly descended over the whole area bringing with it complete silence, no bird noise, no traffic noise, no nothing. As I climbed down from the water tank, I could survey the surrounding area; two or three completed factories and one or two sites being prepared. I could not see any people anywhere. As I walked to the front parapet of the factory roof, I spotted in the far distance what looked like a welding flash, but it was too far away for me to judge the cause. I watched the intensely bright light as it appeared to get brighter and larger by the minute. By now, it looked about a mile away, but I could clearly make out that it was indeed travelling, and quite quickly. I then realised that it was an electric arc travelling down the overhead power lines which ran alongside the main highway down island, which itself was some two hundred metres from where I was standing. I watched the blinding light travelling at speed down the cables hoping that it would carry on past the junction which supplied our industrial area with its power. But it didn't. What caused it to take a 90 degree turn into the industrial area I didn't know, all I knew was that it was heading our way, but looking at the poles carrying the cables, it would still need to make a second 90 degree turn to reach us. I watched spellbound, unable to do anything. I was shouting to anyone on the ground to turn off the factory power supply at the transformers because I couldn't get off the roof quickly enough. The fiery arc reached the second 90 degree tee junction, and I watched in horror as again, for reasons unknown, it leapfrogged to turn left, and it was coming fast in my direction. I was blinded by the light as it ran towards the junction which fed our factory, and I had to crouch down behind the parapet wall so intense was the crackling arc. This is where the dragon dance paid for itself because the arc passed our junction at speed towards our neighbour, a Japanese factory manufacturing scooters and light motorbikes. There was a tremendous explosion as the factory transformers were destroyed, and when the dust settled, I could see that the building housing the transformers was just a pile of rubble. Descending to ground level, I was pleased to see that the power into the factory had been isolated and our transformers had escaped damage. A stroke of sheer luck? Maybe there was something I didn't know about dragons.

Several weeks passed and Tom had not turned up, and I had all but given up hope that he ever would. Then one morning, Sophie, my Manchurian secretary, came into my office to say that there was a fracas going on with our security guard at the front gate, with some undesirable character trying to gain entry. Taking John with me, we arrived at the gate to see what I would describe as a tramp being manhandled by our guard who was shouting at him and pushing him away. John recognised Tom, but I certainly did not. Nevertheless, I took John's word that it was indeed the man I had hired at midnight. We took Tom into the factory, put him through the showers, gave him a clean uniform and haircut, and he emerged transformed as a recognisable employee. What is more he turned out to become a competent high speed wrapping machine engineer.

I was ever aware of the local Chinese ways of 'doing business' and trying to instil western business practices was an uphill task, and many were the times I was solicited for tit for tat arrangements. Nothing of consequence, but I had to keep my wits about me, trying to differentiate between an innocent favour and a loaded one. For instance, I must relate the story of Mr Hsu. He had been awarded the contract of supplying all the factory's printed wrapping and packaging materials. A substantial contract it was, properly quoted for. Mr Hsu was the kind of man you could not fall out with, a most polite and smiley soft spoken man, who ran a good business and provided first class materials. I rarely had need to criticise his supplies, but on the odd occasion it became necessary. Mr Hsu was always immaculately dressed in dark blue or dark grey suits. On one visit to my office however, he turned up in a spectacular light beige suit and as he walked into my office I complimented him, telling him how smart he looked which set him beaming. It was an off the cuff remark as far as I was concerned, but little did I know what I had set in motion. The following morning, I arrived at the factory a little later than usual and was surprised to see sitting on my desk four large bolts of suiting cloth all in light colours. Sophie came in to tell me that I had an appointment to visit Mr Hsu's tailor in Taipei city that afternoon. I told her to call Mr Hsu to tell him that I needed to see him at my office, and indeed he was there the next morning. I tried to explain to him that I could not accept his generosity, but he got very upset saying that he was sorry that his gift was not acceptable to me and that he would get me a better gift. I told him that it was not the company's policy for employees to accept gifts, but he was getting more and more upset, and I thought he was going to burst into tears. I had to make an executive decision and came down in favour of Mr Hsu, who in dollar terms was one of our major suppliers, and I judged that there was nothing to be gained by refusing his offer which, on the face of it, may only send the wrong message to him. The following day was Saturday, and Mr Hsu arranged for me to meet him in the city to attend his tailor for measurements to be taken. I wrongly imagined that we would be attending at one the many excellent tailoring establishments in the city but not so. I was taken to the seedy back streets where foreigners didn't venture. Mr Hsu and I stepped out of the car into a narrow street where children were playing all manner of street games. There were baseballs, footballs and ping pong balls whizzing about, and I was asked to wait while Mr Hsu strolled into one of the tiny houses to emerge with the tailor, a tape measure draped around his neck. Why do tailors of any nationality always look like tailors? I greeted the small man cheerfully and introductions were made. Naturally, I expected to be escorted to his workplace. But no. I was to be measured up in the middle of the street. The children stopped playing games to gather round me in a huddle, laughing and chattering and cheering every time a measurement was recorded. They obviously found me more interesting than their games, I couldn't imagine why. The finished suits fitted perfectly—and Mr Hsu was happy.

I received a telex from the U.S. office telling me that we were to be paid a visit by a consultant hired by them to visit all the companies' factories around the world to train management staff and operatives in the art of 'ELIMINATION'; his patented method of cost saving and improved productivity. I met Earl at Taipei airport to find that his luggage had been lost, and he had reached the frantic stage which was understandable because in those flying days, lost luggage was often not recovered due to rudimentary tracking techniques. Fortunately, he had kept his valuables in his carry on case which included all his technical material, but his day to day clothing and such were missing. We were able to assist with these essentials but had his technical material case gone missing, his whole tour would have been curtailed.

Earl gave his lecture to all staff in the canteen hammering home the basic concept, which was his patent that if you have a problem of any kind at work, be it technical or otherwise, the best solution is to think 'ELIMINATION' that is, don't waste valuable time trying to solve the problem, simply eliminate it and move on. I know that may sound over simplistic, but it did have a value when in the planning stage of any operation, or any personal planning. Ask yourself if you run up against a problem do I really need to find a solution—just don't buy it or repair it or plan it, just eliminate it from your thinking. Earl had made a lot of money selling this revolutionary idea to big business in the U.S. and abroad. I could have applied his concept to the lost luggage, but I'm not that sort of guy. The Chinese however could make no sense of what he was talking about since most of them didn't understand English, and the ones that did also didn't know what he was talking about. After his address, Earl sidled up to me and whispered, "I don't feel that I have got my message across, can I show them a short film illustrating the principle."

"By all means if you feel it would better illustrate your point" was my reply. We had a screen, and Earl had a 35mm film projector, and we set everything up in short time. The film turned out to be a cartoon and illustrated a working office where people were working at desks, but to get a drink or visit the toilet workers would need to leave the office through a door built into a half glassed partition forming a corridor which ran the length of office area. The cartoon people were a bit jerky in their movement, and the Chinese thought it funny because I could hear the tittering going on as the dialogue was in mandarin, and although I couldn't understand it, the Chinese could. It opened with a scene showing a cleaner mopping the corridor in jerky movements, and the mop he was using was small, then after mopping part of the corridor length, there appeared above his head a large exclamation mark—he had an idea. "Why don't I get a bigger mop and I don't have to keep walking back and forth to the mop bucket so often." This he does. Then he gets another idea. "Why don't I bring the bucket nearer to the mop?" Finally, he ends up with a mop so wide that he can't get it into the bucket, and he gets a wider one. Then he realises why he has to mop the corridor so often. It's because the office workers have to walk the length of the corridor to get a drink from the large water bottle so tramping dirt on the corridor floor. So, he gets the door into the corridor moved to be opposite to the water source, and finally he gets the water bottle relocated inside the office. By this time, the Chinese were rolling in the isles with laughter. Every time the cleaner got an idea, the audience clapped and cheered. They thought it was the funniest thing they had ever seen. Earl wasn't impressed at all with the reaction of the

Chinese, but I thought the whole episode turned out to be a stress breaker and from that point of view it was a success. Earl left Taiwan the following day for Australia. Goodness knows what kind of reception he got there, for I knew from experience that Aussie workers do not take prisoners.

Then in 1971, the UK chose to recognise communist China diplomatically to replace the Republic of China as official China which put the cat among the pigeons vis a vis the Tamsui consulate which the Taiwan Chinese were now about to seize in retaliation. The British consul Tom Duffy decided that the locals were not going to confiscate the consulate furniture and works of art and called an urgent assembly of all the Brits on the island where he would auction off to the highest bidder. There was a party atmosphere at the consulate on that day with flowing wine and champagne. Everyone was charged up to strip the impressive consulate building bare. That was the instruction to the fifty or so people there with Tom himself being the auctioneer as bids were bellowed at him from all directions. When we left the scene that day, there wasn't a stick of furniture, a picture or an ornament in the place for the locals to find when they arrived to commandeer, which they did the following day. I got the consul's desk and two fine glass door display cabinets, which just about fitted in Robert's company van he had kindly loaned me for the day. Robert wanted to drive the van himself, but I thought discretion to be the better part of valour to have a local present at a consul sacking. That was the time I became an Australian for a short while when hiring a taxi in town. For a few weeks following the recognition of mainland China, taxi drivers would ask me if I was English in which case he would not drive me. The seriousness the locals placed on this "betrayal" was fuelled in the China Post which daily claimed that Taiwan would eventually take over the mainland governance. It was also said that there was a department within the Taiwan government offices responsible for the planning of such a venture. Chiang Kai-Shek was still lobbing one shell per day into communist held islands off the northern coast to receive one shell per day fired in return just to keep things warm. Technically, I lived next door to Chiang Kai-Shek because my house was half way up the mountain, and the president's palace was at the bottom on the same side with little in between, and on many occasions, I would meet his cavalcade leaving the palace and would need to wait until he was out of sight before the armed guards would let me pass. I was told to be very careful by local residents not to get too near to the palace gates before stopping to let the president's cars move away because his armed guards were triggered happy. Robert told me that on one occasion a coolie working in the paddy fields opposite the palace gates stood up from his planting to wave to his president, but the guards misread his intention and shot him dead.

There was excitement amongst the ex pat community when the first American burger chain, I can't recall the company name, opened for business in Taipei. In addition to being able to eat inside the restaurant, there were and chairs and tables with parasols on the patio in front, all very continental. Naturally, it was well patronised by all the ex pats and the wealthier locals for there was nothing like it on the island at that time. It had been trading for some months and was as popular as ever, when without warning, it was raided in broad daylight by the police. They drove the patrons off the patio and scattered the tables and chairs. The reason printed in the China Post was that it was illegal to be seen eating in public, notwithstanding the fact that locals and expats alike were eating off street food stalls all over the city. There was a suspicion that the burger restaurant was doing so well that it was taking business from the food stalls or more to the point that it was reducing the profits of the money men who owned them.

It was an unwritten law amongst the Euro ex pats that you needed to cultivate at least one American military friend who had access to the USA military PX store in order to be able to buy, occasionally at least, western food delicacies like cheese or marmalade. Butter also if you were lucky. Obviously, these were proxy purchases through the kindness of your friend, as long as you did not tear the backside out of the favour. It was always known by the ex pats when a US supply ship had delivered goodies because you would see Chinese government officials tearing down the Chung Shan main highway through the city with their Mercedes bulging at the windows with new bedding, washing machines and all manner of household items, not forgetting the western food essentials. These 'authorised' officials had first call, along with the senior US army hierarchy, I would assume, to strip the prime items before they would allow the rank and file to enter the store. Lots of these items would appear in the downtown stores for sale at an inflated price, and food items would appear in Suzie's Kitchen also at premium prices. Still the ex pats, especially those with a friend, did benefit by the odd treat, courtesy of the US army so there was little to complain about. The US army every year celebrated American Law Day, and the American school which my son attended ran a competition to judge the essay best describing the American way of life and its benefits and shortcomings relative to the rule of law. Categories based upon age groups could submit an essay, but no name or nationality could be given, each applicant being assigned an entry number. It was assumed, according to my son, that in the senior category, it was the father of the student who would write the essay to be submitted by the son. Not officially of course. I had correctly assumed that the first two prizes from the three awarded would be flag waving efforts therefore I wrote a constructive critique being of the firm opinion that Americans would appreciate the fairness in my essay. They did so, and I won third prize two years in succession netting $50 government bonds in the process. I wish I could find them now for I never did cash them in.

I was summoned to attend a summit meeting to be held at the USA head office with the intention of widening the companies' presence in the fast emerging Far East market. I sat around the conference table with the company top brass firing questions at me relative to my experience on the ground to enable them to assess the possibilities for expansion. One of the more outspoken of the directors asked me what my export quota commitment to the Taiwan government was as a condition to their granting investment approval. I correctly replied, "50% sir."

"So, what did you achieve?" he asked.

"40% sir." Ah hah he sighed loudly.

"You know what you would have achieved Don if you had been an American—50%, because an American would have made sure by booking out as export a couple of containers then hired an out of the way warehouse to keep them in to be shipped out later." Then he let out a loud guffaw, and the rest of the directors put 'know all' smiles on their faces.

"That's how I got my 40%," I said. A short stunned silence followed, then, to their credit, the directors roared with laughter, and the one who challenged me bellowed "Fantastic!" and tossed me a big cigar.

Back in Taipei, it was almost Christmas which was the time that my wife organised her annual medieval evening dinner and gathering of clans held at our house, when everyone had to attend in European medieval dress. Our guests went to extraordinary lengths with their costumes.

We had Alabama Chelsea pensioners, German royal courtiers, crinoline ladies, highwaymen and Jim Nodland. Jim was from Joplin Missouri and was an unforgettable character who worked for a major American electronics company on the island. How his delightful wife Millie went on with him at home nobody knew. Jim was living in a world of his own, a totally placid man—laid back would be an understatement—who did not concern himself with the problems of life—he just ignored them. He was an asset to any gathering so long as there was beer, except during work hours we assume, but otherwise he was never seen without a can of beer in his hand. He would arrive at your front door with one, and he would depart with one, and continuously in between. Everyone liked Jim, and you knew your party had been a success if Jim had passed out twice. He always recovered after the first one, but totally harmless. Millie told the tale of her and Jim being in a bar in Joplin when an inebriated drunk asked Jim what time it was. Jim obliged whereupon the drunk hit him over the head with a bottle. Jim rubbed his head and said to the man, "That was not very nice of you," then ejected him into the street.

One particular Christmas, we planned the medieval gathering as was expected of us, and together my wife June and the in house cook, Didi, had together decided on the feast menu, when my driver Chen out of the blue asked me if we would allow him to prepare and present the feast with Didi as his assistant. At first, I thought he was joking and we laughed together when I told June of Chen's request. He had been my driver for 12 months, and as far as I was concerned he was a very good driver but preparing a feast for twenty or more people was not in his job description, and I told this to him quietly not wishing to hurt his feelings. Then he dropped his bombshell. He wasn't a chauffeur by profession but a qualified sous chef, and he had fibbed in his interview with me because even though he worked at the best hotel in town, he could make more money driving for an ex pat. This went down like a lead balloon with Didi when we told her that she was being usurped by our driver, but we eventually soothed her feathers, and she agreed to play second fiddle. The banquet that Chen prepared having given him carte blanche could only be described as magnificent and would have graced the finest restaurant in quality and presentation—Didi was so impressed that she asked Chen to teach her his recipes. We failed to understand how Chen, with his obvious talent, could not command a higher salary in his profession than he could as a driver. It was six months later that I was forced to dismiss Chen as my driver for fiddling company fuel expenses, and I was in deep trouble with June as a result who thought highly of both his cooking and his driving, and I must admit that I fired him through gritted teeth.

There occurred one incident involving Chen before he did leave my employ which was totally out of character. The company decided to authorise a sales drive which involved customers collecting gum piece wrappers after use and using free application forms available from the vendor, they would be awarded with a camera if they submitted one hundred individual wraps. I hastened to add this was not my idea, but a dictate from on high. The text on the application forms was naturally Chinese character, so I could not read it, but my factory accountant could, and he was responsible for the management of the promotion. Accountant Wong came into my office one morning to say that he suspected that there was a scam afoot, not that I was in the least surprised. He had discovered that there was an unusually high response to the offer emanating from the local Neili senior school—more than three hundred from a school with only one hundred students which dwarfed the response from the rest of the country.

On investigation, it was noticed that the majority of wrappers submitted from the school were new and unused and could have been stolen from the factory store. John Chiang arranged for me to visit the school headmaster to express our concern, and he and I set off one morning to do just that, with my driver Chen at the wheel. John and I sat in the rear seats and were organising our strategy in what could be an embarrassment for the headmaster and indeed to the reputation of the school itself within the neighbourhood. We had our documents and records all sorted out laid on our knees as Chen told us that we were approaching the gates of the school. Chen must have been day dreaming because as we drove between the substantial stone pillars of the opened iron gates at too high a speed, we suddenly found ourselves flying through the air over the school yard. Chen, for reasons unknown, had not noticed the twelve concrete steps leading down to yard level some nine feet down. The car landed with a bang throwing John and I into the front seat, our well organised papers scattered, with arms and legs all over the place. Students who were just emerging from the school ran to help to untangle the mess inside the car. I felt like I had just crawled out from under a rugby scrum, John was badly bruised about his face, and Chen escaped with no more than a tarnished reputation as a driver. All in all, it was not the ideal start to the dressing down I had to deliver to the headmaster. I got to my feet and looked around to see that there was actually no way a car could be driven out of the school yard, the steps being the only way out. Turning to Chen who was too bewildered even to apologise, I told him that if my car was not at the top of the steps when I came out after my meeting, he would be fired on the spot. The Nissan Cedric was a large heavy car, and as I looked at the vehicle then at the steps, I was frankly under no illusions as to the task facing Chen, but the mood I was in was not conducive to forgiveness or helpful suggestions, and I was going to leave the challenge with him. Then I marched into the school with John carrying an armful of loose papers and files behind me.

The headmaster was a quiet studious looking character who greeted us without a word about our airborne arrival as I provided evidence regarding our suspicion of wrong doing at his school. In fact, he seemed so detached from what I was saying through John's translation that I began to think that he had set the scam as a project for the students. He was obviously not going to admit that but did what all heads of departments do and blamed it on his assistant who he sent for. The assistant head came sheepishly into the office where John related in Chinese what we were there for, and he offered no defence, in fact he admitted that he had contrived the scheme together with his students one of whom had an uncle who worked in our stores. No apology was offered, but I now had the name of the uncle and could take the appropriate action. Case closed. Meanwhile in the schoolyard, Chen had commandeered the senior boys to gather around my car and they were trying to manhandle the vehicle sideways up the steps. There was a boy every two feet around the car, plus Chen himself shouting orders. Nearby, there was a crowd of senior girls shouting encouragement to the boys who were moving the car up the steps one by one. It was a precarious operation, for the car was in danger of back sliding every time they lifted step by step but they were close to the top of the steps as we came out of the building, so I did not interfere, though I was concerned for the boys behind the car who were in danger from the backslide should it overcome them. As they dragged the car over the top step, there was a loud cheer and shrieking and clapping from the girls, and I must say that it was some achievement by the boys to whom Chen owed his job. The Nissan suffered no damage that we could see, Chen checked the suspension and the underside of the car and gave it the thumbs up, so away we went to cheers from the students. The incident reminded me that there was no such a thing as a normal day at the office in Taiwan as I understood it.

Robert told me that if I wished to eat good Chinese food at office lunch time, I should go to a certain hotel whose name escapes me, in Neili town. I took his advice and was surprised to find that the hotel restaurant was in fact a small theatre complete with a curtained stage and theatre lighting. During lunch the diners were treated to a full scale revue show with singers, acrobat acts, puppeteers, magicians and Chinese comedians whose jokes were lost on me. I was the only non-

Chinese in the place, and the staff got to know me since I took lunch there most days. Robert was right, they served very good Chinese food, and the daily lunchtime shows were good amateur quality. I learned that such shows were common in many Chinese hotels and that in fact they served as breeding grounds for aspiring actors and performers trying to join the professional ranks. The local patrons would shout at the performers both encouragement and clapping or insults and booing if they didn't like the act. It was reminiscent of old time English music hall, and it certainly brightened up lunchtime.

A representative from a veteran soldiers association visited my office one day to inform me that he managed a veteran's factory in the town which manufactured Chinese carpets and that he would be pleased to show me around if I was interested. No second invitation was needed, and I arranged to meet him there next morning. What a fascinating morning I spent with him and his young workforce. These were children of dead or invalided soldiers who were looked after by the veterans association, housed and fed at the factory, they had bunks to sleep in, and ages ranged from toddlers to teenagers. They manufactured top quality Chinese wool carpets which would grace the finest English mansion, and I commissioned one myself following my tour. The organisation of the children in the numerous stages of production was mind boggling. The youngest working team, ages ranging from 9 to 12 were responsible for the intricate task of hand weaving the various colours of weft into the warp as they sat at intervals on a wooden plank which ran along the face of the warp in front of them. Behind them was an adult who was shouting out pattern instructions to the ten children one by one by colour. It had to be seen to be believed. As the warp moved continuously slowly down in front of the children, they would listen for their instruction, then using a razor sharp spring hand shear, they would pull off a pile length of the correct colour of weft from reels, knot it on to the warp then cut it all at lightning speed. The older teenagers were responsible for the washing and dying of the virgin sheep wool all very heavy work done by hand. Finally, the finished carpet was patterned profiled, trimmed by skilled teenagers using the hand held spring shear. There were toddlers running around the place, some on homemade toddler scooters and bicycles and the whole factory appeared totally shambolic to me, but it certainly produced the most beautiful Chinese carpets sold for high prices in local and overseas markets. Whenever I look at the beautiful carpet they made for me which graces my drawing room, I picture those youngsters sitting on their plank working at lightning speed for their livelihood.

My first impression was that the children were being exploited, but I quickly realised that mothers and children were happy and well cared for and that but for the veterans and their carpets many of them would be destitute and on the streets.

Running the length of Taiwan's east coast is the Chung Yang Shan mountain range, and within these mountains lies Sun Moon Lake and the spectacular Marble Mountains of Taroko Gorge, a must see for ex pats that time, where some roads are solid marble, and the numerous road tunnels through the marble rock glisten in the car headlights in multicolours. Driving along these narrow roads often alongside precipitous drops into the gorges or the sea is definitely not for the faint hearted, and on the occasion that I took my family there, my wife suffered a traumatic experience when we parked our car to walk up to a high pedestrian look out. My son and daughter stayed at the bottom beside the rushing river eating at a snack station while my wife and I climbed the hundred marble steps cut into the mountainside to reach the lookout to admire the multi-coloured marble peaks and boulders as they reflected the rays of the setting sun all along the gorge. It was a magical sight. Then we thought we should collect the children from the bottom of the gorge and make our way home. To reach them we had either go down the steps to the base of the canyon, then cross a footbridge over the river which lead to the recreation area or cross a high level single person width rope suspension bridge, then down steps on the opposite side, which seemed the shorter route. I had spotted a few local Chinese cross the suspension bridge by simply strolling across and said to June that if they could do it, so could we. I went across first, but as I approached the half way mark, I realised that the ropes supporting the wooden slatted walkway which also served as hand rails to hold on to, were below waist high. The long bridge was swaying from side to side as I walked, and the view into the gorge below was truly terrifying. I planned to tell June not to attempt the rope bridge as I thankfully reached the other side, but when I looked around, she had already started across. She got close to the middle walking very slowly then she sank to her knees and froze on the gently swaying bridge. I stepped back on to the bridge which caused it to sway more every step I made. June screamed at me to go back which I did. I was joined by several local ladies waiting to cross the bridge who found it very amusing to see June on her knees not able to move in terror. I dropped to my knees at the bridge entrance and told June to look directly at me and keep looking at me then crawl on her knees towards me and don't look down. Very slowly, inch by inch, she made progress until I could reach her hands and pull her to her feet. The local ladies gave her a round of applause smiling broadly. Then, one by one, they sauntered across the bridge as though it was a walk in the park. The bridge was obviously for locals only and should have carried a hazard warning to unsuspecting visitors.

Chapter Thirty
Unspoiled Pattaya (1966)

Today's Pattaya bears have no resemblance to the quiet almost deserted beach resort which was the escape from Bangkok vital to the ex pats of that era. Sleepy and relaxing, sparsely populated with few man made attractions, it was the water sports and the sailing and the uncrowded beaches which dominated. There was simply nothing else there. I had been living and working in Bangkok for at least four months before. I knew of Pattaya through an Australian colleague who invited me and family to hire a beach cottage at Rock Cottages in preference to staying at the one and only hotel which was over rated at one star. I got cottage seven shaped like a stranded boat with basic facilities but certainly one up on the hotel. Bob was masterful in all the water sports including sailing as you would expect of an Australian virtually brought up on a beach, whereas I had only experience of jumping over the salt heavy waves as they hit the Blackpool beach. No contest really. Bob was determined that I should I should learn being that I was fit and in my prime, in addition to being active in most land bound sports. I could swim in the local public baths, but sea swimming was a different kettle of fish. "Meet us on the beach at six am sharp tomorrow morning. I've hired a fishing boat to take us to the uninhabited island, and we have to catch the tide early" was Bob's last words to me before retiring to our first night in the stranded boat cottage. We made the deadline—just complete with provisions for the day and our two bleary eyed children, but where was the boat? Bob and wife and his two children were standing at the water's edge looking out to sea at a Thai fishing boat some 200 yards offshore waving their arms at a fisherman who was beckoning us to wade out. The four children aged five to ten years old would need to be carried and the four adults shared one each, and laden with paraphernalia we ventured into the clear waters of the gulf. The first 50 yards was easy going in knee high waters, but gradually we were waist deep with a hundred yards to go and the ladies were suffering under the load. Then to make matters worse, we walked into a large shoal of jelly fish which began to sting our legs at which point Bob and I were too compelled to hoist the ladies on to our shoulders so severe was the stinging, and with two children one in each arm the wives on our shoulders carrying miscellaneous necessities, Bob and I struggled to reach the boat. Although the fishing boat had a shallow draft, it was unable to get closer to shore due to being stuck fast on a sandbank we were told, as the two Thais assisted in dragging the sorry lot of us on to the deck. To add insult to injury, as the six of us sprawled flat on the hot decking in exhaustion, we failed to notice that the tar caulking between the deck boards had melted in the blazing early morning sun, and we were all profusely smeared in black tar on our nearly naked bodies. Our trip couldn't suffer more setbacks could it? Our legs were reddened with jelly stings particularly the two ladies who were quite badly stung made worse by being smeared with tar, and we were in further danger of being badly sunburnt since there was no cover available on the boat. Thankfully, we had managed to arrive with two small umbrellas which provided respite for the children, but the adults had to resort to diving into the sea periodically to cool off. We quizzed the Thai captain as to why we were stuck on a sand bank and how soon we could sail on, and did he expect to be paid. He apologised as best he could in very broken English, but we got the impression that Bob knew more about sailing than he did. What he did know was that the tide wasn't due to come in for two hours or so to lift us off the sandbank which set Bob into action mode. He said that he would swim out seawards taking the boat's anchor with him, and he would signal to us when to man the winch and drag us off the sandbank. It was then that the captain told us that he had a small inboard engine which could assist us, and he would start it up on signal from Bob. This lifted our spirits somewhat as Bob, who was a powerful

172

swimmer, dived in clutching the anchor, and myself and the two boatmen manned the hand winch to await Bob's signal. Having reached a sufficient water depth, Bob planted the anchor on the seabed and waved a signal. We started to wind in the rope slack which tightened until the three on the winch were straining to overcome the load. The rope was now so tight that it took all the strength of the three of us just to prevent the winch from spinning in reverse, for there was no safety ratchet to prevent this, and we had to admit defeat. Bob climbed back on to the boat and we had no option but to await the turning of the tide, which when it did occur two hours later, was if a magical unseen hand had gently lifted the craft off the sandbank, and we were away. The sun was high in the sky by the time we anchored off shore of the small uninhabited island as all 'farangs' knew it as, although it must have had a local name, we never knew it. We were the only people there, and we had the whole beach and shallow off shore sea to ourselves. I showed my inexperience by jumping from the boat to be the first one on the beach where the sand was red hot, and I had to retreat post haste.

As we strolled around the beach in our beach slippers, Bob pointed out what he described as a fertility temple. At first sight it was difficult to make out exactly what it was, and the ladies couldn't make it out at all. Time to go snorkelling at which Bob was naturally an expert and which I had never attempted before due to there being no scope for such pastimes in industrial Lancashire. Sharks never crossed my mind, which demonstrates just how green I was regarding the dangers lurking in tropical waters. I didn't encounter a shark fortunately, but as I surfaced from viewing the spectacular coral reef life on what was my first attempt to emulate Bob, I came face to face with a large swordfish cruising just below the surface. Then it was joined by another as we studied each other at close quarters. I looked towards shore and was surprised to see how far away it was, then realised that the tide must have turned, and I made for the nearest rocks. I had never swam that distance before and was exhausted as I clambered on to the barnacle encrusted rocks to gather breath. I couldn't see the boat or anyone in the water, but as I re-entered the water hugging the shoreline, I spotted the anchored boat. I could barely believe how far away I had drifted but after a long slow swim, I re-joined the others who were wondering where I had got to. It was a salutary lesson which I never forgot. We set sail back to Pattaya beach battle scarred and sunburnt, tar covered and myself badly scratched from my encounter with the barnacled rocks. The children had nevertheless had a great time. To round off our initiation into water sports, we encountered an ink black cloud which came in rapidly from the sea and the boat was tossed around like a cork in the high wind and torrential rain. The ladies and the kids were seasick, and having been forced to lower the sail, we were reliant on the small inboard engine to get us to shore which it eventually did, and we waded back to the deserted beach very much the worse for wear. We revisited the uninhabited island and other offshore islands on our many visits to Pattaya, and I'm pleased to say that we didn't revisit the trauma of our first attempt. Still, Bob was determined to convert me to the Australian way of water sports and despite my reluctance to try water skiing and against my better judgement plus the goading from the two wives, I agreed to give it a go. The families watched from shore as Bob settled me in crouch position in the water at the same time instructing me in the art. What happened next I have never been able to live down even though it was 50 years ago. As Bob was instructing me how to take the strain and with me holding the triangular rope handle tightly, a speedboat raced past us some 20 yards away seawards. What I didn't know was that I was tied to it, and I don't think Bob did either. One minute I was talking to Bob, the next I was airborne clinging on for dear life, I was horizontal, but the water skis were vertical. It was some seconds before the tips of the skis hit the water and I did what felt like a dozen somersaults. The small crowd of onlookers on shore cheered and laughed when I eventually broke the surface to find Bob wrestling to release me from the skis in deep water. I was beginning to wonder what the Aussies saw in water sports, but I was definitely made for land sports at which I was pretty good all round. Bob persuaded me to have one more attempt, this time at his favourite past time— sailing. He hired a two man sailing boat, and we set off in fair weather with Bob managing the sail and the tiller. "This is more like it." I told him—"I could get used to this." I was sitting as instructed on the side using my weight to offset the wind direction when Bob shouted ABOUT which meant nothing to me until the sail jib struck me on the side of my head and knocked me overboard. We were a half mile offshore, and when I surfaced, the boat looked very far away. I was wearing a life jacket, but it was of poor quality, and I had to tread water for an age until Bob could manoeuvre the boat back to drag me to safety.

"I thought everyone knew what ABOUT meant in sailing terms," was Bob's excuse.

"Everyone in Australia maybe, but not in Lancashire," I replied. That was the end of my attempts to master water sports, and henceforth I limited my efforts to swimming, sunbathing and watching Bob. I paid the price for my amateurish attempt at water skiing two days later back in Bangkok by being rushed into hospital with severe bleeding in my chest due to a torn muscle. Bob and I remain the best of friends.

Chapter Thirty-One
Gainesville Intercontinental (1987)

I had always harboured a desire to visit the deep South USA to experience the culture and hear country music first hand, and when I was assigned to spend a fact finding week at the company factory in Gainesville Georgia, my ambition was realised. Collected by limo from Atlanta and an hour's drive later, I arrived in Gainesville, a provincial town east of the city and found myself in the almost deserted main street with the driver having made a quick getaway before I could ask him where the hotel was because I could see no hotel in the vicinity. It was a fairly depressing looking high street at first sight, deserted of walkers just a few passing cars. My past experience of Intercontinental hotels was that they were significant in that they were instantly recognisable as a hotel, but I could see nothing resembling such a building. I meandered up and down the street towing my suitcase with no one around to inquire from but apart from numerous burger bars and saloons nothing resembling a hotel, and I was on the point of walking into one to ask where the Intercontinental was when it struck me that the limo driver must have been instructed to deliver me to the hotel, and I returned to my dropping off point. I studied the adjacent roadside buildings one by one and found a small brass plaque which carried a faded engraving Hotel Intercontinental adjacent to which was a scruffy looking large double gate with a personnel door which opened when I tried it. It led into large courtyard car park with what looked like a multi storied back packers hostel at the far end. The whole car park and hotel frontage was decked out with large British flags fluttering in the breeze. Maybe, they know I'm arriving I mused, but they needn't have gone to such lengths. On reaching the reception desk, I was deflated to find that the flags were not due to famous Southern Hospitality but to mark the Gainesville MG motor club show and shindig. The receptionist welcomed me and thanked me for travelling all the way from England to attend the gathering which explained the crowds of men in the foyer and bar. I didn't take a census, but I was probably the only guy there who wasn't in the club but the other attendees refused to believe that I was there for any other reason when I got into conversation with them, particularly when I admitted to having owned an MG Magnette saloon many years ago. The beer was flowing, and some of the more inebriated got word that I was from England when I was surrounded by backslappers who assured me that nobody would come to Gainesville for business or pleasure, so I must be representing MG England. My long journey and not least the boisterous reception took its toll on me, and I was glad to see my bed, in a room that was, to put it kindly, a little below the standard of room one would expect of a real Intercontinental Hotel, but it was clean and adequate. I was to be collected by car at 8:30am the following morning, and it was at the breakfast buffet bar that I made my innocent but fatal mistake. As I lifted the lids on the bacon, the eggs, the sausage tureens and so on, I reached the porridge tureen which I must say was an unexpected surprise, and I helped myself to half a kilo—except that it wasn't porridge it was grits. It was, I thought, a little different to the porridge I was accustomed to, but I, nevertheless, cleared the lot, then I ate a hearty fried breakfast and felt much better—for a while. I never did get into the factory that day.

I felt at home with the Southerners who were friendly and welcoming and who constantly asked me to speak so they could hear 'proper' English as they put it. The trouble was that often I couldn't make out what they were saying due to their extreme Southern drawl. One incident I recall occurred in the factory canteen when I tried to dispense myself a glass of orange juice. I fiddled with the handle, but nothing happened and the queue behind me was getting restless when the lady behind me shouted "Royised levver." I looked at her, and she repeated "Royised levver' I must have had a blank look on my face because she shouted in my face 'Royised levver' and started to laugh. Then it clicked. Raise the lever—of course or lift the handle in my vernacular. On another occasion, I fancied a burger and went into a burger bar and joined the queue. When I reached the front, I was faced with a large black lady who flicked her head to me in inquiry, and I asked her what range of burgers she had since there was no listed menu board. She rattled away in superfast Southern black speak English which was totally unintelligible to me. The man behind me who was also black read my bemused expression and asked if I needed a translation which I gratefully thanked him for amid loud titters from the rest of the queue.

A tour around the town illustrated the abject poverty that many people were living in, far worse than what I expected to see, shocking in fact, and unexpected by me to see in prosperous USA in the 1980s. In contrast, there were also areas of splendid colonial style mansions and stately homes surrounded by large and beautiful gardens which, I suppose, displayed the history of much of the Deep South. All of the people that I met both in business and leisure were polite and helpful, and I thoroughly enjoyed my one and only sojourn to this part of the world.

Chapter Thirty-Two
A Narrow Escape (1977)

Sitting at my desk in the UK a few days before the Easter break, I received an unsolicited telephone call from a London based multinational company who had somehow traced my international career in factory construction and management, and would I be interested to interview for similar project in Iran. At the time I was employed as Production Director to a UK based company and was far from contemplating such a move. However, the terms were attractive enough to cause me to agree to pay a visit to the Iranian site with no obligation, provided that it could be arranged over the upcoming Easter weekend break to allow me to be back at my desk on the Tuesday morning. So it was that I touched down in Tehran mid-day on Good Friday to be met by an Iranian representative of the company, who drove me to the city office to meet the MD and his panel all of whom spoke good English, eventuating in my being offered the job, the only problem being that the factory site was not in Tehran but in Rasht a coastal town on the Caspian sea. "I would need to visit the site before I could consider the offer," was my reply, which was agreed to, and I was to be collected from my hotel at 7am to be driven north to Rasht, a journey of some four hours I was informed. What they didn't inform me was that we would need to drive over the Elburz Mountain range on a single lane barely sealed road, through six feet snow drifts. The car was a Humber Sceptre identical, but of older vintage than the car I was driving in the UK at that time. Had I been aware of the terrain we were about to travel through, I would have challenged the wisdom of making the trip in that car. As it was, we set off and were soon clear of the city limits and through the slum areas into pleasant rural countryside.

One hour passed before we began to feel the effects of the climb into the foothills or more to the point the old car engine was feeling the effects. I was, by now, listening to every gear change, and I didn't like what I was hearing until I was compelled to ask the driver if there was any oil in the engine and gearbox. I regretted doing that because he turned his head away from the road to talk to me, and we narrowly missed an oncoming truck. "I think OK," he said but he didn't sound too convinced.

"Please stop the car and we check before mountain climb," I said as I looked at the snow covered peaks ahead. He pulled off the road and we both got out of the car since I wanted to check for myself. The engine dipstick showed dry, and the gearbox was just showing an oily tip. I waved my arms in front of my chest to signal to the driver that I was not going to proceed into the mountains under those conditions. He just smiled and flagged down a snow covered truck which was travelling in the opposite direction. All the trucks must carry emergency oil because the truck driver offered to top us up from his five gallon can—no charge. Must be a regular occurrence I thought as I thanked him, and it was smiles all round. He only carried engine oil no gear oil, but we were in no position to worry about that. In fact, I was more concerned about the amount of snow covering his truck as the two drivers had a chat, probably discussing the road conditions ahead I thought. On we drove with the noise from the engine abated but only a little, it still sounded very angry. The two lane road merged into single each way, and we really were in the wilds of rocky mountain terrain but as yet clear of snow for which I was grateful. The car didn't like the ever steepening incline at all, and we were travelling in second gear at high revs, and we still hadn't hit the snaking road which could be seen ahead of us. A couple of miles further on, and the driver understeered on a right had bend, and we ran off the road into a huge snowdrift. It must have been the bottom end of an avalanche because we had not encountered snow on the road up to that point. The driver swore in Iranian, but we were well embedded and unable to open the two front doors, so no choice but to clamber into the rear to get out since the engine had cut out and refused to restart. It was only when I stepped out of the car did I realise how cold it was outside, and the two of us were attired in lightweight suits. Where was the passing traffic when you needed it— none in either direction. The driver produced two woolly blankets from the car boot, and we wrapped ourselves in these as best we could. He also produced a small hand shovel, and we took turns to clear the snow from the front of the car to enable us to check the engine which took half an hour or so, and I, for one, was near to freezing solid despite the digging. I must admit that I was losing a little enthusiasm for the job by this time, but I theorised that things could only get better, and I had been told by the driver what a wonderful place the Caspian seaside was to visit, and besides, at that moment, I had little choice but to try to keep from freezing. Opening the bonnet at long last, the driver ascertained that the two carburettors needed to be cleaned out, and he set about doing just that though how he could feel his fingers baffled me. The way he went about the job told me that he had done the same job before. It worked however, and he reversed the car back to the road and the heater gradually thawed us out. Nearing the summit of the climb, the car spluttered to a halt, and on examination, the driver told me that one of the carburettors had collapsed beyond repair and that there was no way that he could repair it and suggested that we should bed down in the car to keep from freezing to death and await a passing vehicle to hitch a lift into Rasht. I was not at all in agreement with this and visualising the engine in my own car in the UK, I hit upon an alternative suggestion which might get us moving. In any case, the chances of hitching a ride seemed remote since we had not met one vehicle on the journey over the preceding hour which was going in our direction.

I was blue with cold as I assisted the driver to re connect the good carburettor to do the work of two. The car started first time, although it laboured to climb to the summit, we made it—just. We coasted downhill into Rasht, and the view was spectacular, so spectacular that I began to believe that despite the tribulations of the journey, it may well have been worth it. The town is set on the coast line of the Caspian Sea amongst heavily forested uplands sweeping up to the snow covered mountains we had just traversed, in a picturesque panorama. The factory was under construction, and there was in fact little to view as far as that was concerned, but there was a site hut office where I met with local officials of the company who frankly did not impress me at all, being aggressive and surly with their anti-western remarks and attitude. It did not take me long to realise that I would need to fire them all as my first managerial act, which probably wouldn't go down very well—and would I be able to get out of the country following. There was a distinct animosity in the air which unsettled me, and although I remained polite, it was a struggle. We did manage to discuss some technical issues amongst the politics, but it wasn't long before I had already made up my mind that the job was not for me or for the family I would be taking along. I was offered a tour of Rasht which I reluctantly declined, and in any case we had yet to make the return journey back over the mountain. The driver had ditched the Humber Sceptre we came in, in favour of a Hillman Hunter which had seen better days, and which I knew had only one carburettor, hopefully in good condition I thought, since we would be unable to repeat the dodgy trick which got us there. The car struggled to reach the summit which must have been the extent of its life as a motor vehicle since it now struggled to motor downhill, and finally it expired in heavy snowfall on an ice covered road surface. The driver managed to slither off the road and plough into our second six feet high drift which stopped the car in lieu of the useless brakes. At least we were still physically undamaged, and we had not gone over the edge which the slithering car had threatened to do so on a couple of occasions. The driver started to mutter in local dialect, and I hoped he wasn't praying. We both wore lightweight business suits, and I had a short raincoat on, but we were totally inadequately clothed to be sat in a car in a snowdrift at the top of a mountain, and as best I could, I had a go at the driver for not taking proper precautions for what he must have known was a hazardous journey. That didn't help matters, but I felt better afterwards. It was still daylight but only just, and we just had to sit tight without the blankets which had been left in the car we had ditched in Rasht and hope that another vehicle would turn up which it did one hour later, a heavy truck going in our direction and which, noting our predicament, stopped, then two heavily built men came to our car and clearing snow from the windows saw us huddled inside and started to clear the car of snow with small shovels. They let us sit in their truck with the heater on while they physically dragged our car backwards out of the drift and lifted the bonnet to examine the engine. What they did to that engine I never knew but using their tool kits, they eventually got it to start. They were brilliant, and though I was unable to communicate with them, I believe that they understood the thanks that I gave them in English when I shook their hands as we parted. They drove their truck slowly down the mountain behind us as we eventually reached fine and warm weather at the foothills.

The following morning at the hotel I met up with the owner and his officials to summarise probably the most challenging interview I had ever attended. They offered me very generous terms and said that I could live like a king in a palatial house with its own lake and wild boar shooting forest. Frankly, I would have been more concerned about what the company car was like. However, I said that I would discuss with their London office to give my decision because inwardly I was unsure of what the reaction would be if I refused the offer point blank, since they had the look of a mafia mob about them. I admit to feeling somewhat insecure until I sat in my seat on the aircraft the following morning.

Subsequently, back in my UK office the following morning after the hottest Easter weather on record, I sat round the board table with my fellow directors sporting their deep suntans with myself lilywhite by comparison fingering my frostbite, we exchanged pleasantries and got on with business as usual. The irony of this story is that six months later, the revolution to unseat the Shah of Iran occurred which confiscated all foreign assets in the country. Amongst them was a massive investment by the UK Company I was with, crippling it financially and causing its demise. For me it was indeed a godsend that I had made the decision I did, not to reside with my family in Rasht, beautiful as it undoubtedly is, despite the palace, the lake and the wild boar.

Chapter Thirty-Three
Always Drive on the Left (1985)

I was hosting a small group of American visitors around my dining table and following after dinner drinks in the subsequent relaxed atmosphere, I was singled out for attack regarding the English institution of driving on the left, and why instead did we not adopt the far more sensible USA right hand rule. They ridiculed our 'roundabouts' and right hand car drivers position complaining that when they drove in England, it was chaos, loudly echoed by the whole assembly. I had to think of a repost quickly to defend the honour of my country, and providence provided when I pointed out to the invaders a plaster frieze on the wall of the stylish dining room we were in. The plaster embossed frieze depicted a Roman horse drawn chariot at full charge with the single soldier aboard holding the rein in his left hand and striking with his sword using his right arm. I stood and quietened the hullabaloo by announcing that driving on the left was the common sense convention to adopt which enabled Britain to conquer Europe long ago who were driving on the right. A hushed silence descended as I explained the reasoning. If you control the reins with your left arm, you could drive your chariot (wagon or car) close up to the bank or wall to prevent an attack from your left while allowing you to strike at your enemy with your natural right sword arm who would be trying to strike cross handed because he would be driving on the right. It took a few seconds for my explanation to sink in before the gawping and bemused Americans erupted in laughter when they realised that they had been snookered. Fortunately for me, there were no left handers at the table.

Chapter Thirty-Four
What About the Children?
(1965)

Today it is difficult to comprehend the magnitude of the then seismic decision I made in deciding to embark on what was about to be 30 years of moving my family from country to country with limited knowledge of what that entailed. When I recall the moment now, I shudder to think how little we did know of the world outside of our immediate Lancashire area surrounded by family and friends where we led the typical parochial lifestyle of the area and were happy and contented to do so. The status quo which had dominated the lifestyle of the area for generations was the coalmines and its associated support industries. All this had recently imploded in short time due to Thatcher's vision of the future, and although I had fortunately found reemployment, I believe that the shattering of so many peoples' security and lifestyles around me did much to embolden me to think outside my usual box. The new job offer I was then considering, which would ship us to places unknown, was tagged to attractive terms of employment which I confess also played a part in my decision to accept—but what about the children aged eight and three. June and I came to the conclusion that we would take them along to wherever we were posted and furthermore that they would not be sent to boarding schools but would be educated within the country we happened to be residing in, despite my contract providing for boarding school fees, which we converted to paying for the best locally available schools in whichever country we resided. My children went to English, American, Australian, Chinese, Philippine and Thai schools, sometimes needing to switch from one to the other. It could have fallen flat, for it was an admitted risk, but it paid off handsomely. We all as a family discovered our hidden talents in one way or another and found ourselves able to exploit and rely on the values taught to us in our family upbringing to best advantage.

We both, to this day, readily acknowledge the debt we owe to the upbringing we received, for I doubt that we would have survived without it. My three-year-old daughter was speaking fluent Thai to the household staff in short time and played with our cook's four year old son who was smaller than she was such that she would carry him around the house tucked under one arm. She also spent many nights sleeping in the servants' quarters although she had her own en suite bedroom as did we all. In 1965 en suite bedrooms in Lancashire were a rarity indeed, but when we returned to take our first home leave break, it was the first thing my five year old daughter demanded and was quite miffed when I told her that we all shared the family bathroom. In all of the countries we lived in, we were lucky to find good house staff who we treated well and who repaid us in kind. We were indeed lucky in this respect for many of our contemporaries were not so lucky, and we heard of a few horror stories. We have never had need to regret our decision to keep the children with us on our wanderings, for both children have retained strong family ties and have achieved success in their chosen careers.

Chapter Thirty-Five
An Invite to Lunch (1998)

It is of no surprise to be invited out for lunch when conducting business, though personally I accepted very few such invites, preferring to conduct business in my office and avoid the inevitable overeating and certainly drinking which neutered any meaningful afternoon work. However, I did receive a verbal lunch invitation on one occasion from Serah, my housemaid, who I had recently found work for in the factory as a trainee machine operator. The invite included my wife and my two young grandsons who were holidaying with us at the time and was for the upcoming Saturday at her home in the Nairobi suburbs. My first instinct was thanks but no thanks, as all sorts of reasons why not ran through my head, but I delayed declining immediately taking time to think about it. We knew Serah quite well, she having worked as our housemaid for the previous three years and an excellent worker she was, disciplined and hard working. In fact, her husband had replaced her as cleaner and gardener looking after our needs at Serah's request and it surely would be woe betide him should he fail to meet with the standards we required. Peter was a qualified tailor and in addition to attending to our tailoring needs, he did the house cleaning plus the gardening plus all the other jobs required around the house, but Serah remained as his—shall we say— incentive to maintain standards. At month end pay day Peter would immediately purchase twelve concrete building blocks which he would lay to the foundation of the 'house' he was building on a small piece of land he owned. Had the invitation come from anyone else, I would surely have declined, but June agreed with me that we should make the effort since we didn't want to disappoint Serah or indeed to appear aloof.

As we drove slowly through the eastern suburbs of Nairobi through narrow streets which were not frequented by Discovery Land Rovers, we had collected a posse of excited youngsters running behind smiling and waving until we reached Serah's house, escorted to the gate by the posse who swarmed on to the car as we parked. I dusted the small children off the car with a large yellow dust cloth and knocked at the gate. We were greeted by Serah who introduced us to her extended family, and we all squeezed into a dimly lit low ceiling room, with hardly room to move. We managed to squat on low benches close to a stack of plates and utensils. The Kenyans were all singing songs of welcome, clapping and smiling, very happy that we had accepted their invitation. It was all very primitive in a way, but the sincerity of the welcome was obviously genuine. There was wood fire burning on the floor in one corner, most of the smoke passing out via a hood and pipe through the concrete roof. Plates of steaming meats were brought into the room and handed around in very cramped conditions. Serah had prepared mountains of all kinds of foods, some we recognised, some we didn't, but she had gone to, what was for her, great expense and we felt humbled at the effort she had made. There was a lot of singing and attempts at dancing in the crowded room, and a good time was had by all. Our two grandsons were overawed by the fuss the Kenyan ladies were making of them, and they stayed close to us. Above all, it was apparent that we had honoured Serah and her family in the eyes of her community by accepting their hospitality which was gratifying to us.

The effect that the experience had on our two grandsons was summed up by the nine-year-old who grasped my hand as we walked to the car, looked up at me and said in a serious tone, "Grandad, I'm going to start working hard at school from now on." I wielded my large, yellow duster to clear the car of small children, and we drove slowly away from the waving Kenyans.

Chapter Thirty-Six
Spooky

Two incidents occurred at the termination of our wanderings for which I can provide no rational explanation and I am not given to fanciful thoughts—quite the opposite. The first incident could likely be explained away as pure coincidence, the second one still leaves me bewildered when I recall it.

I was packing up the children's mountain of toys tossing away the damaged and tattered items and collecting the still usable toys into large black bags as we prepared to leave our Bangkok house to travel on to Manila. Sitting on the bedroom floor, I was being ruthless in my choice from the heap of stuff at my elbow relishing the opportunity to get rid of some accumulated rubbish.

Doc Rabbit My five-year-old daughter had a soft toy, Doc Rabbit, from the cartoon character 'What's Up Doc' cartoon film. There was pull ring in its back which when pulled caused the rabbit to clearly speak one of six recorded sayings. I had heard them all while playing with my daughter—'good morning how are you.' or 'have a nice day' and the like. The rabbit was in a distressed condition having been well misused, in fact my daughter had discarded it some time ago. I picked it up and threw it across the room on to the scrap heap. To my utter amazement, the rabbit said clearly 'take me with you' without the pull ring having been pulled, and not having said that before ever in the time we had had it. I looked at the rabbit staring at me for a second or two a bit nonplussed, but what else could I do but take it along.

Truly Weird We had arrived back in the UK from an overseas assignment, and my adult son was staying with us over the weekend. On the Friday evening, my son announced that he had a bell ringing engagement at a church some 12 miles distant. The January weather was foul, heavy driving rain and gusty winds causing us to try to persuade him not to attempt the journey in his small car, but to no avail, since he did not want to let down the rest of the bell ringing team. By 12:30 am he had not returned, and we were getting quite worried since the storm had intensified, but eventually retired for the night leaving all outside lighting on. At 1:30am we were very worried about his safety, no mobile phones then, when suddenly we heard the front outside door open and close with a bang. The house at that time was under internal renovation, and the stairs and landing were uncarpeted, so we clearly heard the heavy tread of our 18 stone son as he stomped up the stairs across the landing, then the distinctive noise made by the turning of the ceramic door knob to the adjacent bedroom. Now fully relaxed and relieved, we slept soundly.

The following dawn, I took a morning drink to my son's bedroom, knocked on the door and entered to find an unoccupied room in which the bed had not been slept in. Just then the telephone rang which was my son telling us that the storm was so bad that he had been forced to stay over at a fellow bell ringer's house. I am very far from being a superstitious character, but for the life of me, I would have sworn on oath in court that my son would have been in that bedroom so clear and unequivocal was the evidence.

Obituary

As I complete this series of true stories, I have just been informed of the death in Bangkok of my loyal friend Pirawatt Panthawi aged 74. He will not be forgotten in this household.

Pele to Conquerer